Filippo Pedrocco

Ca' Rezzonico
Museum of 18th Century Venice

Marsilio  MUSEI CIVICI VENEZIANI

complete guide

MUSEI
CIVICI
VENEZIANI

Photographs by
Francesco Turio Böhm, Venice

Photographic referencies
Musei Civici Veneziani, Museo Correr
photographic archive p. 8,9

Translated by
David Graham

Cover
Giandomenico Tiepolo, *Mondo novo*,
detail

Graphic design of the guide
Tapiro, Venice

© 2005 by Marsilio Editori® s.p.a.
in Venezia
First edition: April 2005
ISBN 88-317-8739-x

www.marsilioeditori.it

Contents

Baldassare Longhena
Ca' Rezzonico, facade

The story of the palazzo

Between the seventeenth and eighteenth centuries:
construction of the palazzo

The story of the construction of the building now universally known as the Ca' Rezzonico is fairly complicated and was quite drawn out, stretching to more than a century.

The area where the grand marble mass of the Ca' Rezzonico now stands, on the right bank of the Grand Canal between Rio di San Barnaba and Calle Bernardo, was occupied until the mid-seventeenth century by two houses owned by the noble Venetian Bon family, which lived in one of them and rented the other. They are clearly visible in the perspective plan of the city published by Jacopo de' Barbari in 1500. Documents of the time describe these houses as being in a state of absolute decay, one 'gloomy and without sunshine', the other 'very, very old' and in need of 'extensive repair'. It was Filippo Bon, son of Ottaviano and head of the branch of the family known as 'di San Barnaba' from their place of residence, *procuratore 'de Citra'* and man of considerable education, who in 1649 decided to make a start on the construction of a new residential *palazzo*, more in keeping with the family's grandeur than the old, dilapidated house they then lived in. The task of designing the new building was entrusted to **Baldassare Longhena** (1597-1682), the designer of the revolutionary 'rotunda' of the Chiesa della Salute and undoubtedly the greatest exponent of Venetian baroque architecture, also in the field of civil construction.

Longhena began construction of the new *palazzo* starting from the area occupied by the two houses, on the bank of the Grand Canal, and by 1661 these had already been incorporated into a single building, where the Bon family took up residence. The Grand Canal facade, though limited in height to the present first *piano nobile* of the building, must have had the same form as that which is still preserved, as can be seen by comparing it with the 1709 engraving by Vincenzo Coronelli showing the state of the building after works were interrupted in 1682. Furthermore, a drawing in the Gaspari collection at the Museo Correr in Venice of the water entrance shows a planimetric layout quite like the existing one, with the only variant being the presence of two well-heads against the side walls in the entrance hall now occupied by marble benches.

Longhena had evidently mainly taken the model of Jacopo Sansovino's Ca' Corner, called Ca' Granda, into account when conceiving the facade. He tried to adapt the triumphal architectural vocabulary of the sixteenth century to the private building of the new century through a very subtle play of typological and stylistic citations, also taken from other celebrated architecture of the past, including the

Palazzo dei Dolfin and the Libreria Marciana by the same Tuscan architect. The seven axes of the rusticated ground floor are separated by Tuscan half-columns and pilasters supporting a plain architrave; there are three openings in the centre, of which the middle one is slightly wider than the side ones. The same definition is repeated on the *piano nobile*, marked though by Ionic columns.

The works were extended to the rear of the building after 1661 and, precisely in order to facilitate construction, in 1667 the *Giudici del Piovego* allowed Filippo Bon private use of the quay on the Rio di San Barnaba, whose ending was also partially incorporated into the new building. Bon also purchased a house that faced onto this quay at the same time. It was then immediately demolished 'to make the new edifice of his mansion'; and the following year he signed an agreement with his neighbours, the Bernardo, for the construction of a spiral staircase. This still exists on the north side of the *palazzo*, jutting out from the main body of the building. The few other notices so far discovered dating from before 1682 concern the purchase of other small houses and bare land needed to unify the area on which the back of the new *palazzo* was being built.

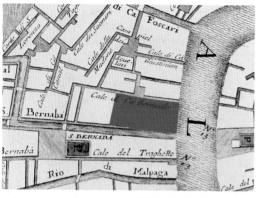

Ludovico Ughi
Map of Venice, detail

**Antonio Canal
called Canaletto**
View of the Grand Canal
detail

As mentioned, building work continued until 1682, when Longhena died. The state of the facade, built only up to the height of the first *piano nobile*, is documented by numerous views by Canaletto, Marieschi and other contemporary artists, who showed it incomplete, with a temporary saddle-back roof consisting of planks of wood. Indeed, the considerable costs sustained in building the new *palazzo*, which Filippo had intended would be the crowning glory of a century of successful business and the tangible sign of his family's importance, had ruined the Bon family and Filippo himself was forced to close the building site, being unable even to provide for the maintenance of the constructed sections, which began to rapidly deteriorate.

On his death in September 1712, ownership of the building passed to his sons Giacomo and Alessandro and, when the latter died in 1744, to his sons Pietro I and Pietro II, also known as Filippo. Unable to resume works or even to simply rectify the deterioration, they decided to sell the building as it was. Interest in its purchase was immediately expressed by Giambattista Rezzonico, the head of a very wealthy family, originally from Lombardy, that traded in fabrics and owned a bank. A branch of this family had moved to Venice at the end of the sixteenth century from a hamlet bearing the family name on the northern shores of Lake Como. On 17 May 1687, the

Rezzonico, who at the time rented a *palazzo* owned by the Fontana family in San Felice, were also admitted to the Venetian nobility. They were one of the many families that, starting from 1648, had been able to buy patrician titles by making large payments into the Republic's coffers, emptied by the ongoing costs of the war against the Turks.

In 1745 the architects Giovanni Sola and Paolo Tremignon were appointed to make a first valuation of the building. They completed this in April of that year and suggested a value of 46,666 ducats. But no immediate agreement was reached between sellers and buyer – there being a series of old inherited encumbrances on ownership of the building – and in 1750 the two architects were called on to make a new appraisal. This resulted in a considerable reduction in the value of the building, now set at 40,611 ducats, due to the 'subsequent deterioration since 1745'. In any case, the sale price agreed on by the Bon brothers and Giambattista Rezzonico was 60,000 ducats, as shown by the purchasing deed drawn up on 3 August 1750 by the notary Francesco Domestici. The *Provveditori di Comun* then ordered a new valuation, from the *proto* Antonio Mazzoni, who in his conclusions emphasised that the building, although having the 'grandeur of an outstanding *palazzo*', was to be considered a 'disastrous, impractical building in constant, imminent danger of collapse', particularly due to the state of the beams, now rotten as a result of the continuous penetration of rain water, made possible by the collapse of the temporary roof and the lack of windows, which had never been fitted. Mazzoni's valuation also confirms that only the rear of the building, completed up to the second floor, had a definitive roof, which by now was also in a state of absolute decay, and that only some of the rooms at the back of the building had flooring in terrazzo, while the wooden planking alone had been laid in the others.

In order to rectify this disastrous situation and to complete construction, Giambattista Rezzonico appointed **Giorgio Massari** (1687-1766), the most celebrated architect then working in Venice. He was famous for having designed the splendid Chiesa dei Gesuati and that of the Pietà, and had for two years been engaged on construction of the new Grassi residence at San Samuele, on the opposite bank of the Grand Canal to the Ca' Rezzonico.

Massari immediately started restoring the sections that had been built and completing the building, and by 1752 the works must have been quite advanced: on 5 August the noble Pietro Gradenigo noted in his diary that 'quite a number of builders, who in the early hours of the day were fashioning a window jamb in the highest part of the palatial restored Palazzo Bon at San Barnaba, bought by N.H. Rezzonico, were unable to hold up the marble stone and, the frame-

View of the room

overleaf:
Gaspare Diziani
Triumph of Poetry
ceiling fresco

39

the energy of the famous singer's irrepressible personality to emerge. But beyond her ability to closely observe the psychology of her subjects, in these works Carriera demonstrated the refined quality of her spirited pictorial language, enlivened by a characteristic, sparkling chromatic tone. The portraits of *Giambattista Sartori* and *Lucietta Sartori* at the bottom of the next wall, dating from December 1737 according to the inscription on the back, are also by Rosalba. Giambattista and Lucietta were among the painter's most faithful friends and Giambattista's sister, Felicita, was one of her numerous students and assistants; the airy autonomy of the brushstroke in the two portraits, informal in the pose of the figures and the clothing, shows the importance Rosalba's relationship with her brother-in-law, the celebrated painter Gian Antonio Pellegrini, had in the development of her expressive forms. Finally, the two miniatures on ivory – possibly the bases of snuff boxes – displayed between the portraits of the Sartori depicting a man (the scholar Anton Maria Zanetti according to some) and a lady, are also by Carriera. They are some of the more interesting examples of the intensive miniature production to which the artist dedicated herself in the early years of her career, achieving considerable success, being nominated a member of the Accademia di San Luca in Rome in 1705.

The other portraits in the room are also of considerable interest. According to an ancient tradition, accepted by the critics, the series of four oil portraits around the one by *Rosalba Carriera* herself, on the wall beside the entrance, showing *Gerolamo Maria Balbi*, his wife *Cornelia Foscolo Balbi* and their children *Marco* and *Caterina*, is by

Gian Antonio Lazzari
Portrait of a Child

Rosalba Carriera
Portrait of Faustina Bordoni Hasse

Rosalba Carriera
Portrait of a Gentleman in Red

Marianna Carlevarijs, the daughter of the Friuli view painter Luca and pupil, as indicated by the sources, of Rosalba. The age of the people represented suggests that these paintings date from the early 1740s. Their derivation from Rosalba's models, though translated with a more incisive graphic sign and colder colouring, is evident in the repetition of the poses and the intimate characterisation of the figures.

Gian Antonio Lazzari, the 'amateur' painter traditionally regarded as one of Rosalba's teachers, is a little-known artist and the three portraits in pastel shown here – of a *Gentleman*, a *Lady* and a *Child* – are the only examples of his work to have come down to us. Their provenance from the painter's heirs and the attribution given in the old inventories of the Musei Civici are, however, a good guarantee of their attribution. There are quite evident similarities with the youthful works of his more famous student in the pictorial layout and arrangement of the figures.

Above the miniatures by Rosalba is a fine pastel portrait by **Lorenzo Tiepolo**, Giambattista's son and assistant, of his mother, *Cecilia Guardi Tiepolo*, dating from 1757 as written on the back beside the artist's signature. This refined painting, marked by delicate shaded tones that are an evident tribute to the manner of Carriera, is one of the first works by the then 21 year-old artist. It is a precious and important foretaste of his subsequent work in Madrid, where Lorenzo followed his father in 1762 and remained until his death in 1776. Between the windows is the big *Portrait of Gian Rinaldo Carli Rubbi*, who was appointed professor at Padua University in 1745 and died

Rosalba Carriera
Portrait of Sister
Maria Caterina

Rosalba Carriera
Portraits of Giambattista
and *Lucietta Sartori*

Lorenzo Tiepolo
Portrait of Cecilia Guardi Tiepolo

in 1749 at the early age of 29. This is undoubtedly a memorial work painted by **Nazario Nazari**, with typically elegant, shaded forms.

The furniture in the room consists of Venetian-made, gilt, carved pieces from the middle of the century. Notable among these is the console-table with onyx top between the windows – on which two allegorical statues in gilt wood, from the same set as those in the preceding room, and a clock in Empire style by **Alessandro Bertolla** are displayed – and the other table in the centre of the room with a marble top. The furnishings are completed by four, richly worked corner stands, a sofa and eight armchairs dating from the same period. The wooden wainscot is painted in tempera with decorative elements imitating those of Tiepolo inspiration in the Nuptial Allegory Room and dates from the second half of the eighteenth century, as does the fine Murano crystal chandelier with its 16 lamps.

Marianna Carlevarijs
Portrait of Gerolamo Maria Balbi

Marianna Carlevarijs
Portrait of Cornelia Foscolo Balbi

Marianna Carlevarijs
Portraits of Marco and *Caterina Balbi*

5. The Tapestry Room

This room takes its name from the three large tapestries on the walls, of Flemish production from the end of the seventeenth century, on which episodes from the biblical story of King Solomon and the Queen of Sheba are narrated with great representative effect and attention to detail. These, along with the magnificent piece of gilt carved furniture, came from the Palazzo Balbi Valier in Santa Maria Formosa.

The furniture consists of two tables topped with green marble (one wall model surmounted by a rich mirror with crest, and one in the middle of the room), six armchairs, a rare three-seater sofa, two consolles, two stands and pelmets for the curtains. The expert craftsmanship, graceful lines and quality of the gilt work make this one of the most notable sets of Venetian-made furniture in rococo style to have come down to us intact.

The ceiling fresco (restored in 2004, with a contribution from Veneto Banca) with its interesting colouristic style depicts the *Triumph of the Virtues*. The Virtues reappear in the monochrome figures on the corners of the false architecture at the base of the fresco. Elsewhere, elegant putti play with each other and with animals. Its attribution to **Jacopo Guarana** is confirmed in the painter's biography included in the *Compendio delle Vite de' Pittori Veneziani Istorici* edited by Alessandro Longhi and printed in 1762, which states that Guarana distinguishes himself by painting in fresco as seen in a remarkable ceiling in Ca' Rezzonico painted with a lifelike delicacy that cannot be bettered in oil'. It is in any case one of his first Venetian works, carried out immediately after his return from a youthful trip to Bologna. Indeed, it is no mere chance that the composition of the Ca' Rezzonico fresco seems to recall examples of Emilian baroque, seen by the young artist during this visit.

The yellow lacquered door with chinoiserie deserves particular attention. It is the only one of three which still existed in the *palazzo* at the beginning of the twentieth century that can now be admired in the building. Sold with the rest of the furniture prior to

View of the room

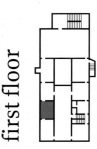

first floor

44

1935, it was generously donated to the Gallerie dell'Accademia di Venezia by an American collector who had in the meantime obtained it and subsequently left it on deposit at the Ca' Rezzonico. Each side of the door is divided into two sections, each containing an oriental scene painted in gold and brown. On the side visible to the public, the upper section shows a Chinese man on a camel accompanied by two servants, while the lower panel features an opium smoker resting lackadaisically on a cushion outdoors, also attended by two servants. The upper section on the inner side shows an elegant Chinese lady protecting herself from the sun with an umbrella and accepting homage from a man on bended knee. The lower section shows a Chinese man seated on a rock with a servant offering him a cup and another sitting at his feet. The main scenes are surrounded by big bunches of coloured flowers and green branches, joined by yellow and pink ribbons, constituting an additional elegant decorative element.

This extremely rare example can be dated to around 1760. Some critics have also suggested that the design may have been provided by Giambattista or Giandomenico Tiepolo, who in this period were working on the frescoes in the *palazzo*.

Seventeenth-century Venetian Art
Three-seates sofa

Seventeenth-century Flemish production
Tapestry with the *Story of King Solomon and the Queen of Sheba*
detail

overleaf:
Jacopo Guarana
Triumph of the Virtues
ceiling fresco

This bright, plush room, upholstered in modern red velvet, faces onto the Grand Canal and the Rio di San Barnaba and takes its name from the rich throne to the left of the entrance in gilt carved wood, with putti, nymphs and sea-horses, dating from about 1730. According to tradition, and confirmed by the writing on the shell held by the putti at the top of the seat back, it was used by Pope Pius VI on 10th March 1782 when he stayed in Chioggia on his way to Vienna as a guest in the *palazzo* of the Grassi family.

The original use of this room is not known. We can only assume that, given its location in the building, it was intended for entertainment purposes. Eighteenth-century accounts say that it was furnished as the bridal chamber on the occasion of the wedding of Ludovico Rezzonico and Faustina Savorgnan in January 1758.

The ceiling fresco represents the *Allegory of Merit* and was painted during the last months of 1757 by **Giambattista Tiepolo**, assisted by his trusted *trompe l'oeil* painter, **Gerolamo Mengozzi**, called **Colonna**, from Ferrara, and his son **Giandomenico Tiepolo**. Merit, depicted as an old bearded man crowned with laurels who ascends towards the Temple of Immortal Glory, is accompanied by Nobility (the winged figure, holding the spear) and Virtue (the richly dressed figure on the right of the old man). Other allegorical figures and the usual repertoire of flying putti surround the joyous procession, while Fame blows her trumpet. The connection with the Rezzonico family is evident in the detail of the winged putto beneath the figure of Merit, who holds the Golden Book of the Venetian Nobility in which the names of the families able to boast the title of Venetian patricians were inscribed. This title was conferred on the Rezzonico family in 1687. The preparatory drawing for the fresco is also known, held in a private collection.

The big cornice beneath is also decorated with several representations of the Virtues. This is probably the work of Giandomenico, as suggested by the more realistic style than in the other figures in the fresco.

The whole allegorical interpretation can be reconstructed thanks to a rare poetic composition by the Paduan abbot Giuseppe Gennari, who had it printed on the occasion of the Rezzonico-Savorgnan wedding. It was intended to exalt the moral and civil virtues of the inhabitants of the *palazzo*, in line with a custom much in vogue in Venice during the eighteenth century. Giambattista managed to avoid repetitive formulas typical of this type of subject and, again inspired by his preferred master, Paolo Veronese, to offer us an excellent work, all based on a sumptuous colouristic style and astonishing compositional inventiveness. The tempera decoration of the wooden wainscoting, with scrolls and figures of old men, would also seem to be a Tiepolo invention.

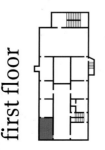

first floor

Antonio Corradini
Detail of the frame *for the*
Portrait of Pietro Barbarigo
by Bernardino Castelli

overleaf:
View of the room

Giambattista Tiepolo
Allegory of Merit
ceiling fresco

The rich gilt furniture in the room is of particular note. It originally belonged to the Barbarigo family before being inherited by the Donà dalle Rose family – with the exception of the throne, which is said to have come from the Grassi home in Chioggia. It consists of four high-backed chairs covered in modern red velvet, a console table, six lamps, two stands, some pelmets and two vase stands, as well as the impressive frame containing the *Portrait of Pietro Barbarigo* painted towards the end of the 1770s by the Treviso artist **Bernardino Castelli**.

This group of furniture has traditionally been attributed to the Este wood-carver **Antonio Corradini** who worked in Venice until the end of the 1720s (he was also appointed by the Republic to supervise the decoration of the last Bucintoro, launched in 1729). This attribution seems in keeping with the conception of this highly elegant set, if

51

not with the actual crafting of the pieces, perhaps entrusted to the master's workshop. There is no doubt that the throne – though of different origin – came from the same workshop.

The wall table is particularly significant. The astonishing quality of the caryatids and the vivacious putti playing with one another between volutes and blooming festoons make this one of the finest examples of Venetian rococo furniture. On its top there is a *Portrait of a Prelate*, in bisquit from the Venetian **Cozzi** workshop.

The monumental carved gilt frame above it was given to Pietro Barbarigo by Count Perulli – undoubtedly along with all the furniture – in thanks for assistance received in a judicial case against the Venetian exchequer. It is easy to assume that the frame originally contained a different portrait dating from the same period (about 1730), subsequently damaged and replaced with that of Castelli on which the inscription recording the occasion of the gift is written. This is confirmed by the fact that the painting was adapted to the frame during the nineteenth century with the addition of two large sections of canvas at top and bottom, where the dedication, evidently repeating the original one, appears.

The frame has a luxuriant allegorical decoration based on the *Iconologia* by Cesare Ripa, a kind of manual of symbolic images that was very well-known in Europe in the seventeenth and eighteenth centuries. Starting with the Barbarigo coat-of-arms at the top, flanked by two angels probably symbolising *Fame* and *Virtue*, and proceeding in a clockwise direction, the illustrations can be identified as: *Love of the Homeland*, represented by a female figure in a cuirass, who is holding two crowns between her hands and treading on weapons while looking fearlessly at the fire and smoke coming from the brazier on her left; *Charity*, a slender female figure with the flame of zeal blazing on her head, surrounded by three children; *Perseverance*, embracing a column and grasping a sword despite the fire enfolding her hand; a putto demonstrating the traditional attributes of *Magnanimity*: the crown, the horn of plenty and the lion; *Prudence*, with some of the objects that make up her vast symbolic repertoire: the helmet, cuirass, mirror, book and serpent; *Justice*, with sword and scales; and *Faith*, a veiled woman carrying a cross, a Bible, a chalice and the symbolic branch of martyrdom.

The glorification of the Barbarigo family, which is obviously the general meaning of this iconography, is announced through three pairs of figures on the same level. In the upper section (*Love of the Homeland* and *Faith*), the Barbarigo are commended for their loyalty to the institutions (State and Church); in the middle section (*Charity* and *Justice*) for their social and civic virtues; in the lower section (*Perseverance* and *Justice*) for their moral character.

A big portrait of the *Nobleman Gerolamo Maria Balbi* dressed as a *provveditore generale da mar*, a post he held from 1751 to 1753, by the Venetian portrait painter **Fortunato Pasquetti**, hangs above the red Verona-marble fireplace between the windows overlooking the Rio di San Barnaba. A large white Chinese vase with gold decorations stands between the windows overlooking the Grand Canal. The two smaller, blue, gold-decorated vases beside the throne on gilt stands with the heads of monsters in oriental style are also Chinese.

The Tiepolo Room is on the other side of the portego.

Fortunato Pasquetti
Portrait of the Nobleman
Gerolamo Maria Balbi

57

The third of four ceilings by **Giambattista Tiepolo** in the Ca' Rezzonico can be admired in this room: a shaped canvas portraying *Nobility and Virtue Defeating Ignorance*. Unlike the frescoes in the other rooms on the first *piano nobile*, this work was not originally in the building but painted between 1744 and 1745 for Pietro Barbarigo to be hung in his family's main *palazzo* in Santa Maria del Giglio. It passed on by inheritance to the Donà dalle Rose family before being bought by the *Venice City Council* in 1934 and placed in a specially prepared stucco frame in this room which, like all the others in the north wing, was originally without fresco decorations. It was restored in 2002 thanks to the contribution of the Leo Schachter Art Foundation.

Tiepolo took up an allegorical theme in this canvas that had often been used for his noble Venetian and Milanese clients, who liked it particularly because of the self-celebratory meaning it implied. The splendid, richly dressed figures of Nobility and Virtue stand out against the bright sky above a cluster of silvery clouds. They are surrounded by the usual repertoire of delightful winged putti, while two very elegant page boys hold the train. Ignorance, dressed in dark tones contrasting with the regal splendour of the clothes of the other figures, is falling downwards, while a cherub, who has snared the bat, her symbol, falls with her. It is evident from Tiepolo's vivid tones and iconographic choices that he has here fully assimilated the teachings of Veronese. However, the intense sensuality of these figures is entirely eighteenth century. In particular, it is easy to see realistic, stupendous proof of the artist's inimitable portrait skills in the care with which he has drawn the facial features and elegant clothing of the page boy holding the train. The model in this case would seem to have been his son Giuseppe

Giandomenico Tiepolo
Old Man with a Crown

Giandomenico Tiepolo
Young Man with a Helmet

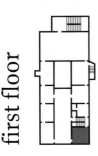

Maria, the future Somaschan priest. There is a preparatory sketch for the central part of this canvas in the Poldi Pezzoli Museum in Milan.

Various other paintings are displayed in the room. A *Portrait of the Architect Bartolomeo Ferracina*, painted by **Alessandro Longhi**, son of Pietro, the most celebrated Venetian portraitist of this period, hangs higher than the others on the wall to the left of the entrance from the portico. Eighteenth-century documents mention two portraits of the celebrated architect by Alessandro: the first was painted in 1758 and the second in 1777. The one shown here, in wich Ferracina is portrayed with the 'tools of his trade', is undoubtedly the later one. Indeed, in the writing at top right Longhi gives himself the title of 'Academicus Venetus', which he was only able to boast from 1760. So this was probably painted from memory immediately after the death of Ferracina in 1777, with the aim of celebrating

Giambattista Tiepolo
St Martin of Tours

Giambattista Tiepolo
St Blaise

the man and his work carried out for the Serenissima. This also explains the particular emphasis in the inscription, where the architect is remembered as 'Novus Archimedes'.

Lower down is a pair of small devotional paintings attributed to **Giuseppe Angeli**, the most trusted of Piazzetta's associates, with images of *St James and St Roch*. These can be dated to the last years of his work with the maestro, around the 1740s.

At the sides of the big bureau-trumeau are two ovals depicting *St Martin of Tours* and *St Blaise*, from the Scuola Grande della Misericordia. Most recent critics agree that these are early works by **Giambattista Tiepolo**, painted in 1715-16, at the same time as the first over-arch decorations for the Chiesa dell'Ospedaletto, of which they repeat the confident, rapid pictorial work and strong colour tones.

On the next wall, at the sides of the big gilt fireplace mirror which almost reaches the ceiling, are four 'fanciful heads' by the school of Tiepolo. The two on the right of the mirror, the *Young Man with a Helmet*, and the *Old Man with a Crown*, are by Giambattista's elder son, **Giandomenico Tiepolo**, and date from the years when he most closely followed his father's style (1750-60); the two on the left are to be attributed to the debut of his younger son, **Lorenzo Tiepolo**, due to the more insistent drawing and brighter colours.

Finally, a picture of *St Paul* hangs between the windows overlooking the Grand Canal. This can be attributed to **Giambattista Canal**, a painter who worked in the Venice region during the nineteenth century, repeating the patterns of Tiepolo and Piazzetta in both canvases and frescoes.

The furnishings in the room comprise several pieces of diverse origin and considerable artistic value: the impressive walnut root bureau-trumeau with mirrored doors and frieze decorated with engraved glass placed in front of the windows overlooking the Grand Canal is possibly originally from the *palazzo*, as shown by documents from the early nineteenth century. In terms of size, quality of craftsmanship and state of preservation, this is a unique example of its kind. It can be dated to the mid-eighteenth century.

The big card table with green cloth top and eight carved legs ending in lion's feet in the centre of the room is also notable. This fine example of Venetian baroque furniture, probably dating from the end of the seventeenth or beginning of the eighteenth century, features wood grain on the legs that has been painted by hand.

A cabinet fitted out as a chest stands against the wall to the left of the entrance, beneath the portrait of *Ferracina*. This is from the seventeenth-century German school (Augusta) and stands on a table with baroque volutes of a later period. The inside of the cabinet is decorated with mirrors painted with animals and flowers and the allegorical representation of Peace.

The furnishings are completed by eight carved chairs in boxwood and upholstered in red tissue, previously owned by the Correr family. These were traditionally attributed to Andrea Brustolon but, given the inferior quality of the carving and the effect that is less monumental than that of the former Venier examples in the Ballroom and the Brustolon Room, were probably made by the workshop or an imitator.

The big, white, Chinese porcelain vase with gold decorations matches the one in the Throne Room. The two marble busts used as decorations above the door are rather the work of an anonymous eighteenth-century Venetian sculptor. Finally, four, fine, gilt, three-armed sconces are displayed on the walls.

Eighteenth-century doors in stamped leather, originally in the Palazzo Carminati, San Stae, have been adapted for this narrow passageway leading to the library. The tempera-decorated cabinets, also eighteenth-century, hold several examples of the rich eighteenth-century collection of porcelain kept in the museum.

The first cabinet is dedicated to the work of the Venetian **Giovanni Vezzi**, who was credited with bringing to Venice the chemical formula for making porcelain, discovered by an alchemist in the service of the court of Dresden, Johann Friedrich Böttger. His factory was established in 1720 and closed in 1727. In this short time Vezzi produced a considerable number of objects, particularly tea services and, in lesser number, vases, plates and coffee-pots. They were distinguished by a hard, translucent finish, quite similar to what was made in the Meissen factory in Saxony, from which the types of objects and partly their decoration also derived. Notable among the works displayed here are the elegant bell cups decorated in iron-red and in blue and gold with mythological scenes, probably by the same **Ludovico Ortolani** named in documents as a decorator at the Vezzi factory, and the splendid globular teapot, decorated with festoons of iron-red plum flowers.

The second cabinet has some examples from the factory of **Geminiano Cozzi**, of Modena, active in Venice from 1764 until the early years of the following century. Typical of this factory was its ability to

Geminiano Cozzi workshop
Tray with blue and gold decoration

Geminiano Cozzi workshop
Coffee and tea service with monochrome and iron-red decorations

continually update forms and decorations on the basis of fashions and changing tastes. The splendid service donated to the Ca' Rezzonico in 1938 by Prince Umberto of Savoy, consisting of a coffee-pot, teapot, tea caddy and cup and saucer, finely decorated in iron-red monochrome with landscapes and scenes of rural life, worthy of a Zais or a Zuccarelli, dates from the early production by Cozzi (one of the pieces is dated 3 August 1767). The other works, some of which are decorated with chinoiserie patterns, are later.

A small canvas portraying the *Martyrdom of St Eurosia*, the young Spanish woman of noble family who was decapitated by the Saracens because she refused to marry a commander from their army, hangs between the windows on the wall in front. The painting was part of the engineer Gatti Casazza's collection, donated to the museum in 1962. At that time it was attributed to Giambattista Piazzetta and only later placed among the works of **Giulia Lama**, due to the anguished quality of the chiaroscuro and the typical formal distortions that typify the work of this important artist. She was the only woman in the eighteenth century to successfully paint historical and religious works, also on a large scale.

Giovanni Vezzi workshop
Bell-shaped cups with iron-red, blue and gold decoration

Geminiano Cozzi workshop
Cups and saucers decorated with coat-of-arms and gold border

Giovanni Vezzi workshop
Plate with blue and gold decoration

A study has been reconstructed in this room with four, impressive, late seventeenth-century library cabinets in walnut. The interesting collection of eighteenth- and nineteenth-century glass objects bequeathed to the museum in 1962 by the collector Gatti Casazza, originally from Ferrara but Venetian at heart, is displayed inside the cabinets. The fine walnut lectern and leather chests displayed between the cabinets are from the same collection.

The furnishings are completed by four simple chairs upholstered in

Antonio Corradini
Veiled Woman

Mattia Bortoloni
Allegorical Triumph
detail of the ceiling fresco

gilt leather painted with floral motifs in the *cuoridoro* (gold leather) fashion typical of Venetian craft. The splendid marble head of the *Veiled Woman* is by the sculptor **Antonio Corradini** from Este; exhibited on a plinth, it probably represents *Purity*. With great technical virtuosity the sculptor manages to make the marble seem transparent and to depict with extraordinary precision all the details of the beautiful face that emerges from beneath the veil. The work is untoubtedly a religious allegory, but the sculpture conveys the fresh, sensual image of a remarkably beautiful young woman, making it difficult to discern a non-profane meaning.

A big, early eighteenth-century turret clock from the **Williamson** workshop in London stands between the windows.

A shaped canvas in a special stucco frame portraying an *Allegorical Triumph* has been adapted for the ceiling. Critics agree that this is by the Rovigo artist **Mattia Bortoloni**, a pupil of Antonio Balestra and painter of numerous frescoes in Venice and the Veneto, Lombardy and Piedmont. The canvas shown in the Ca' Rezzonico has a busy composition of not easily interpreted allegorical figures. It certainly represents the triumph of the royal figure shown in the centre, surrounded by Merit (the old man crowned with laurels dressed in white and yellow clothes in a lower position than that of the king, with two putti holding the open book at his feet), the imposing winged figure of Fame, on the left, seen from behind as she blows her trumpet, and that of Faith (or, less probably, Chastity), the winged figure at top left, almost painted in monochrome, as is the scene below the figure of Merit with two women assisting an old invalid, probably alluding to Charity. The notable plasticity of the figures and the use of a marked chiaroscuro that distinguish this work confirm its attribution to the young Bortoloni, comparable in its composition, the morphology of the figures and the harsh chromatic range, to the frescoes painted in 1716 in the Villa dei Cornaro in Piombino Dese.

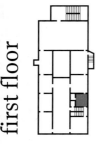

This communicating room owes its name to the nineteenth-century attribution of the three big mythological canvases on the walls: at that time all were believed to be by Lazzarini, a Venetian painter who was active between the end of the seventeenth century and the first decades of the eighteenth, now mainly noted as having been Giambattista Tiepolo's first teacher. Subsequent studies have actually shown that only the one portraying *Orpheus Slaughtered by the Maenads*, on the left of the entrance, is by **Gregorio Lazzarini**. It was painted in 1698, as documented by contemporary sources, probably commissioned by the nobleman Vettor Correr. The smaller canvas between the windows relating the story of *Heracles Spinning in Omphale's Palace* is more likely to be by **Antonio Bellucci**, dating to immediately after his return from a trip to Vienna in 1702, while the third, showing a *Battle between Centaurs and Lapiths* of great dynamic and dramatic tension, is certainly by **Antonio Molinari** and probably contemporary with that of Lazzarini. These three paintings of equal height originally furnished the portico in the San Stae home of the abbot Teodoro Correr, whose bequest to the city in 1830 made up the original nucleus of the Musei Civici Veneziani collections.

The ceiling consists of five ovals in gilt frames that stand out against the deep blue background. This series of ceiling canvases was also not originally part of the Ca' Rezzonico furnishings, but was moved to the museum in 1936, along with the one now in the Brustolon Room, from the Palazzo Nani on the Rio di Cannaregio. It seems that these were originally a single decorative unit, possibly in one of the Nani family's country villas, which was only subsequently divided and adapted to decorate two different rooms in the main family seat in Venice. The ceiling now in the Lazzarini Room was in a first floor room.

Antonio Bellucci
*Heracles Spinning
in Omphale's Palace*

Antonio Molinari
*Battle between Centaurs
and Lapiths*, detail

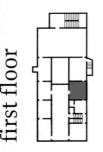

Francesco Maffei
Prometheus with the Mirror and the Eagle

Gregorio Lazzarini
Orpheus Slaughtered by the Maenads

The five ovals are to be attributed to the seventeenth-century Vicenza painter **Francesco Maffei**. In the centre is the figure of *Prometheus with the mirror given to him by Minerva and the eagle*, which is probably an allegory of Sight, to which the attributes of the mirror and eagle allude; it is surrounded by those of *Daedelus and Icarus, Prometheus Unbound by Heracles, Perseus showing the head of the Medusa to Atlanta to punish him*, and *Andromeda tied to the rock* being saved from the monster thanks to the intervention of Perseus. These paintings, of considerable pictorial quality, are fine examples of the lively, baroque-style decoration typical of Maffei. They can be dated to 1657-8 on the basis of their stylistic similarity to known works by the Vicenza master from that period, evident in the brownish shades, the grandiose creative impetus and the marked play of chiaroscuro.

In the centre of the room there is a splendid desk in precious wood veneer with inlays in carved ivory and rods in gilt bronze, made by the renowned Turin cabinet-maker **Pietro Piffetti**, signed and dated 1741 in the scroll on the back of the central section.

Notable among the other furniture in this room in particular are the four simple seats upholstered in leather painted with allegorical figures. Two large wall tables in walnut and an elegant settee with openworked back in elegant rococo style complete the room. There are two big nonces framed in stucco with three cast-iron arms on the walls.

The 'decorative furnishings' carved by **Andrea Brustolon** for the Venier family, displayed partly in this room and partly in the Ballroom next door, are unanimously considered the greatest masterpiece of early eighteenth-century Veneto woodcarving. They were completed in 1706 – the date that appears, along with the artist's signature, on the back of the base of a statue portraying an *Ethiopian Warrior* – for the *portego* of the Palazzo di San Vio where the nobleman Pietro Venier lived. They subsequently passed by inheritance to the branch of the Contarini family known as 'degli Scrigni' in 1758 and in 1841 were donated to the Accademia di Belle Arti before reaching the Gallerie dell'Accademia in 1895. From here they were moved to the Correr Museum in 1911 and have been exhibited in the Ca' Rezzonico since 1936. They consist of 40 quite different items. The most famous is undoubtedly the console vase stand depicting the *Allegory of Strength* on the lower section. Strength is personified by Heracles, vanquisher of Cerberus, the hellish three-headed hound, and the monstrous Hydra of Lerna, shown straining to hold up a rudely worked top with his club and mighty shoulder. The top is carved in the form of a real, rough-hewn tree trunk on which lichens sprout and the marks left by the woodsman's axe can be seen, with a group of three nude black boys in ebony chained together in the centre holding a stand on which a large vase rests.

Andrea Brustolon
Ebony and boxwood chair

Andrea Brustolon
Allegory of Strenght

overleaf:
View of the room

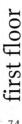

Two bearded old men sit lower down beside them holding two vases each. Their figures are a direct citation of the river divinities sculpted by Gianlorenzo Bernini for the fountain in Piazza Navona, recalling Brustolon's youthful stay in Rome.

This piece, like the others in the set, is notable for its imaginative conception and exceptional craftsmanship. The whole work is played out on the chromatic contrast between the different components: the gleaming, almost metallic black of the ebony, the warm red-brown of the boxwood and the dazzlingly bright white of the original Chinese and Japanese porcelain vases decorated with ethereal designs and chinoiserie.

Antonio Bellucci
Portrait of Procurator

The load-bearing structure of the twelve monumental chairs that are part of the same group is also in ebony and boxwood. No two of these are the same. Brustolon unleashed his imagination in the invention of different legs and crosspieces reproducing branches of trees, and especially in the splendid figures, arranged like caryatids on the upper parts of the front legs or on the arm ends where they join the backs.

The backs and seats are upholstered with late seventeenth-century panels in small stitch embroidery with big medallions framed by volutes with leaves and flowers. The back panels carry allegorical figures within extremely realistic landscapes, while those on the seats show exotic animals arranged in imaginary scenes.

The same exceptional virtuosity of craftsmanship is also apparent in the splendid series of vase stands that complete the Venier supply. Here Brustolon gave a further example of his inexhaustible creative imagination. There are 25 pieces, each one quite different: nine chained, nude, black boys, caught in various attitudes; two caryatids in ebony with eyes in glass paste, a Moor, also in ebony, carrying a boulder on his head and on which a vase rests; allegories of the Four *Seasons* (*Autumn* symbolised by an inebriated Bacchus, *Winter* by an old man seen from behind warming himself at a brazier, *Spring* by a young girl, also from behind, with a crown on her head and receiving flowers from a putto, and *Summer* by a young woman with a wheatsheaf) and the *Five Elements* (*Air* and *Water* symbolised by young beauties, *Fire* by Vulcan, *Earth* by a man with a lamb at his feet and *Light* by Apollo, the god of light); finally, there are two groups of putti arranged in a pyramid on top of sea monsters from the deepest recesses of the oceans and two pedestals for vases decorated in relief with seahorses and putti intent on play.

Several paintings of considerable interest are also displayed here, all from the seventeenth or early eighteenth centuries. At the centre of the wall to the left of the entrance from the Lazzarini Room is the *Allegory of Fortitude* by the French-Belgian painter **Nicolas Régnier**, in Venice called Niccolò Renieri, originally in the Palazzo Vendramin Calergi; the canvas depicting *Pandora*, attributed to the same Flemish painter, who was active in Venice from 1626 until his death in 1667, is a precious example of his refined but lively palette. The next painting, of *Lot and his Daughters*, is by **Pietro Ricchi**, known from his city of origin as il Lucchesino and who was a person of some importance in the sphere of seventeenth-century Veneto painting. *Tantalus Unchained*, attributed to the Genoese painter **Giambattista Langetti**, hangs above one of the two elegant architectural cabinets with statues in gilt bronze with tortoiseshell inlays and, respectively, the coats of arms of the Gradenigo and Contarini families. The leading exponent of the late seventeenth-century Tenebrist style, Langhetti was active in Venice after the middle of the seventeenth century and gained particular success with his intensely dramatic pictures, in the style of Ribera, marked by a heightened display of sentiment.

The big portrait of a *Procuratore* above the grey-pink marble fireplace (owned by I.R.E.; it belonged to the renowned collector Germanico Bernardi) is a fairly problematic work. It was previously attributed in the old museum inventories to the Friuli artist Sebastiano Bombelli and to the workshop of Bernardino Castelli, but is now better placed among the early work of **Antonio Bellucci**, with a date of 1685-90. It shows an unknown Venetian procurator, sumptuously dressed in precious, fur-trimmed crimson velvet, who seems to have just got up from the armchair behind him and is making a polite gesture towards a newly arrived guest. Further back, beyond the plinth of the column, a marble statue can be seen showing a woman presenting a ring. This is probably an allegorical representation of Marital Fidelity, whose presence could be explained by the reference to the unknown procurator's recent wedding. Indeed, despite the official nature of the dress, the portrait tends mainly to highlight the more intimate aspect of the subject's personality, pictured in a kindly attitude inside his own home.

There is another much discussed work on the wall towards the Ballroom, a *Rape of Europe* variously assigned to Gregorio Lazzarini or Francesco Trevisani. However, attribution to a non-Veneto painter – possibly from Emilia – is not to be excluded, given the cold tones of the colouring and evident references to the world of Cignani.

The two paintings flanking the splendid *Allegory of Strength* by Brustolon are rather the work of **Jacopo Amigoni**. They relate the stories of *Judith and Holofernes* and *Jael and Sisera* in tones of dark delicate colours that contrast emphatically with the drama of the biblical events recounted. They were probably painted by Amigoni after his last return to Venice in 1739 from travels that took him to most of Europe, when his palette became brighter and more refined.

The ceiling decoration consists of eleven canvases of different shape and size which, along with the five now in the Lazzarini Room, may originally have been part of a decorative set painted by **Francesco Maffei** for a country villa owned by the Nani family, subsequently separated and recomposed in two different rooms of the family seat in Cannaregio. The four monochrome tondi at the corners of the ceiling representing the *Four continents*, though, are by a different hand. These, too, are from the Palazzo Nani and were in the past thought to be the work of Gerolamo Brusaferro. Recent documentary discoveries, however, show that these canvases were painted by **Francesco Polazzo** during 1765, probably in order to integrate Maffei's decorations when the canvases on the ceilings of the two different rooms were separated, when all the works by the Vicenza painter also underwent significant enlargements and alterations.

The overall iconography of Maffei's paintings, certainly dating from 1657-8, like the others in the same group, is difficult to read. In the centre is the oval with *Jupiter*; the other three ovals around it presumably show the *Allegory of the Senses* (Smell, Touch and Hearing; but Taste is missing); *Diana and Saturn* are shown in the larger elliptical quatrefoils, with *Mercury and Venus with Cupid* in the smaller ones. Finally, *Apollo, Mars and Divine Wisdom dressed as Minerva* (holding the book with the seven seals) are shown in the smaller tondi.

Although it is almost impossible to completely interpret the complicated iconographic meaning that inspired the painter, the quality of the impetuous paintings is in any case quite clear and they are properly considered by critics to be on a pictorial par with the facade of San Moisè.

The stupendous crystal chandelier shines at the centre of the room with twenty lamps in two tiers, decorated with elegant flowers in polychrome glass paste. It was made around the middle of the eighteenth century in the Murano works of **Giuseppe Briati** and is certainly the most extraordinary and innovative example of its type to have come down to us intact.

The portego on the first floor is reached by going back through the Lazzarini Room.

Jacopo Amigoni
Jael and Sisera

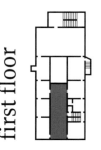

The *portego de mezo* is the wide corridor that normally connects the canal entrance to the land entrance on the ground floor of Venetian *palazzi* and is repeated on all the upper floors, acting as a communicating space for the rooms facing onto it. The *portego* is traditionally decorated with frescoes or big canvases in stucco frames. Such was also the case in the Ca' Rezzonico, as shown by eighteenth-century documents, with four canvases of religious subjects by the Neapolitan Luca Giordano, removed in the nineteenth century. With the original paintings lost and the stuccoes deteriorated, it was thought appropriate to alter the appearance of the room during the restorations carried out prior to the opening of the museum in 1936, resulting in the walls being given a pink marbling finish, which can still be seen. The room is decorated with a group of eighteenth-century marble busts, portraits and allegorical figures over the doors, placed on shelves and in specially made niches, some of which are by the Bassano sculptor **Orazio Marinali**. The furnishings consist of four big portico sofas in elegant rocaille style, distinguished by the stylishly vibrant design of the back which is repeated beneath the seat, and six stands in walnut with hunting and biblical scenes carved on the top, possibly of Spanish origin, from the end of the seventeenth century. An elegant, eighteenth-century, gilt sedan upholstered with red silk is also on display.

An altar piece showing *Mary Magdalene at the Foot of the Cross*, painted for the Chiesa delle Terese in 1663-4 by **Giambattista Langetti**, is displayed on an easel. This is one of the first works painted in Venice by this Genoese artist who was destined to become the leading exponent of the Tenebrist style. In this painting, however, the Ribera-like 'atrocity' that was to mark his subsequent work is toned down by the delicate chromatic effects.

The monumental doorway leading to the stairway to the second *piano nobile* is in the form of a triumphal arch and has the Rezzonico coat-of-arms at the top with the family motto inscribed in gilt letters: 'Si Deus pro nobis'. The doorway is certainly based on a design by **Giorgio Massari** and dates from the time of completion work on the *palazzo* carried out by this architect in the 1850s. The head of a youth on the keystone seems to be from the workshop of the classicist **Giovanni Marchiori** who, along with Gian Maria Morlaiter, frequently worked with Masari. Two vigorous sculptures by the sixteenth-century artist **Alessandro Vittoria** have been placed at the

sides of the doorway. These were originally fireplace telemons, but were subsequently altered to become figures of Atlas by the arbitrary addition of two celestial globes.

The portego on the second piano nobile is reached by ascending the staircase, where marble reliefs of different periods can be noted on the walls of the landing.

Giambattista Langetti
Mary Magdalene at the Foot of the Cross

View of the portego

83

second floor

The most important paintings owned by the museum are displayed in the *portego*, in keeping with the typically Venetian use of the 'picture gallery'.

The following description is clockwise, from the left of the entrance. The first painting is an invented view by the Friuli painter **Luca Carlevarijs** – signed 'L.C.' on the crate being fastened by two men on the right – noted mainly for his numerous views of Venice painted from the early years of the eighteenth century. However, most of his work

as a view painter took place alongside his work on real or imaginary landscapes. This *View of a River Port* is a fine example of the latter, painted shortly after his return to Venice from Rome and therefore datable to the first years of the eighteenth century. The painter has here assembled architectural motifs gathered from various places in the papal city. The arched bridge could be one of those over the Tiber, perhaps the Ponte Rotto, the equestrian monument is based on Bernini's *Constantine* and the houses in the background are a partial view of the Isola Tiberina. Although Carlevarijs was not interested in the precise representation of reality in this work as he was in his subsequent Venetian views, but rather assembled elements from life in an imaginary

Antonio Guardi
Portrait of Marshall Matthias von der Schulenburg

whole, the elements typical of his mature work are already evident, particularly in the central section with the quay flooded in sunlight and the lively characters painted in bright colours.

Alongside is an *Architectural Caprice*, a replica of a painting given by Canaletto to the Venetian Accademia di Pittura e Scultura in 1765 in homage for his admission as a perspective teacher and which is now displayed in the Venetian galleries. Of all the numerous known replicas of this painting, the Ca' Rezzonico canvas – once owned by the noble Sceriman family, who subsequently donated it to the congregation of the Carità – has the greatest pictorial quality. Its attribution to Canaletto is quite certain due to the precise similarity of technique and execution to the late works known to be by the celebrated Venetian view painter.

The next painting depicts a *Diplomatic Meeting*, painted to commemorate the commercial agreement signed at the Hague between Holland and the King of Naples on 27th August 1753. An important part in this was played by Count Finocchiatti, who also commissioned the work and appears in it twice: on the right as he enters the

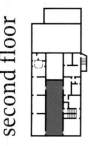

Luca Carlevarijs
View of a River Port

Giambattista Piazzetta
Death of Darius

87

room accompanied by his councillors, and seated at the head of the table on the left while taking part in the talks. The names of the other participants are listed on the scroll on the right, next to the door, which carries numbers referring to the individuals. This is therefore a series of portraits, probably taken from engravings or graphic records.

The painting has in the past been variously attributed to Alessandro Longhi and to Gian Antonio Guardi. Only in recent times does it seem to have been correctly placed among the youthful works of

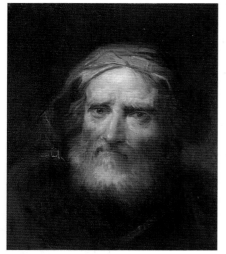

Giuseppe Nogari
Head of a Old Bearded Man

Francesco Guardi, along with other interior views, including the more well-known *Parlour of the nuns of San Zaccaria* and the *Ridotto in the Palazzo Dandolo at San Moisè*, also on display in the Ca' Rezzonico, with which it makes up a matching set, though having a slightly different chronology.

On the opposite wall, to the left, hangs the *Portrait of Marshall Matthias von Schulenburg*. This is one of at least twenty portraits of the commander of Venice's land troops, documented as having been painted by **Antonio Guardi** – for many years his preferred artist – between 1737 and 1742. Inspired by the courtly tradition of European portrait painting, and in particular by a model by Van Schuppen, this work is mainly notable for its chromatic quality, the sudden flashes of light illuminating the battle scene in the background, of great representative immediacy, and for the detailed and incisive portrayal of the facial features.

Alongside is a big canvas showing the *Death of Darius*, painted around 1746 by **Giambattista Piazzetta** for the hall of the Palazzo Pisani Moretta in San Polo, where it was accompanied by a painting by Paolo Veronese depicting *Alexander and the Family of Darius*, taken to the National Gallery in London during the nineteenth century. This is one of the masterpieces of the historical genre mainly cultivated by Piazzetta in his later work. An intensely dramatic work, marked by an exceptional maudlin tension, it shows examples of great pictorial skill in the overall plotting of the scene, in the statuesque figure of Alexander and in the abandoned bodies of the Persian king and his horse, all touched by a leaden light.

A painting by **Gian Antonio Pellegrini** showing *Mucius Scaevola before Porsenna*, from the Istituto delle Penitenti (owned by I.R.E.), hangs here in a modern stucco frame. This is a fine example of the mature work of this great exponent of international rococo, all centred on the quality of the bright colour and a light, softened design. The painting probably dates from the years between 1706 and 1708, when the artist painted the large *Generosity of Scipio* for the Palazzo

Corner in San Tomà, now in Newport, which has very close colouring and lexical similarities to the Ca' Rezzonico canvas.

It is followed by two early masterpieces by **Canaletto**, the *View of the Rio dei Mendicanti* and the *View of the Grand Canal from Ca' Balbi towards Rialto*, acquired by the Comune di Venezia in 1983. These are the only paintings by Canaletto that can be admired in the city's public collections.

The two big scenes were part of the von Liechtenstein princes' collection in Vienna in the late eighteenth century, along with two others (now in the Thyssen collection in Madrid) of almost identical size depicting *St Mark's Square with the Basilica in front and the Grand Canal seen from San Vio towards St Mark's basin.* They represent the greatest achievements of the artist's youthful period, painted in the years immediately after his stay in Rome from 1719 to 1720, when he decided to abandon his work with theatre scenery (which he had been making until then in the employment of his father, Bernardo) to dedicate himself to the painting of views. The example of Marco

Gian Antonio Pellegrini
Mucius Scaevola before Porsenna

89

Ricci, the Belluno landscape artist who also worked as a scenographer and whose work Canaletto had certainly observed closely in his formative years, was of fundamental importance in his first attempts in this field.

The precise dating of these views is controversial. Nevertheless, some elements within the individual paintings would seem to allow this to be fixed with some precision in a fairly broad period of time, to the first half of the 1720s. In *The Grand Canal seen from San Vio*, in the Thyssen collection, it is possible to see the scaffolding that was erected at the end of 1719 for reinforcement work to the dome of the Chiesa della Salute. Given that Canaletto certainly returned to Venice in 1720, it is conceivable that this painting dates from close to that time. *The Grand Canal from Ca' Balbi towards Rialto* exhibited in Ca' Rezzonico makes a pair with the Thyssen painting, given the evident similarity of style. Indeed, they are identical in terms of the perspective, with the view taken from a fairly high elevation, the accentuated theatrical emphasis of the rather small figures, the warm, dense colour reflecting the lessons of Marco Ricci and the use of artifice to bring a vast area of shade into the foreground. This latter is cast with quite singular contrivance – certainly a result of his scenographic experience – by buildings on opposite banks of the Grand Canal, therefore using diverse light sources, almost as if two opposing suns were shining at the same time.

The third painting in the series, *St Mark's Square with the Basilica* (Thyssen collection), undoubtedly dates from 1723-4. This is confirmed by the stage reached in laying the new trachyte and Istrian stone paving in the square conceived by Andrea Tirali. The *Rio dei Mendicanti* in the Ca' Rezzonico may be regarded as contemporary with this or slightly later on the basis of its evident stylistic similarity. The tone of colour is less contrasted in these two paintings, anticipating the luminosity of works dating from the second half of the 1720s, such as the *View of the Campo dei Santi Giovanni e Paolo*, now in Dresden (1726 c.) or even the very first canvases painted at the same time for Consul Smith. The figures have partly lost the forced interpretation seen in the early Canaletto paintings; they are described with greater accuracy and their importance in the context of the whole work is more evident, given their greater and more correct dimensions with regard to the architecture.

Some works by artists trained in the workshop of Giambattista Piazzetta are displayed on the short section of wall beyond the door to the Guardi Room. In the middle is the *Communion of St Philip Neri*, by **Giuseppe Angeli**, to whom Piazzetta had entrusted the direction of his workshop. This painting can be dated to around 1760, with the characteristic clear, powdery colours that reappear in Angeli's work after his teacher's death in 1754.

Canaletto
View of Rio dei Mendicanti

Canaletto
The Grand Canal from Ca' Balbi towards Rialto

Fracesco Zuccarelli
Landscape

Giuseppe Zais
Landscape

Marco Ricci
Landscape

Marco Ricci
Landscape

93

On the left of the Angeli painting are two examples of **Domenico Maggiotto**'s work: at the top a *Boy with Apple* and beneath a *Boy with Fife*. This second work in particular, datable to around 1740, is notable for the fineness of the chiaroscuro and the elegance of the chromatic range. At bottom right is a *Virgin Reading*, a partial copy of a painting by Piazzetta held in a private Roman collection, probably by **Francesco Cappella**. Above it is a *Head of an Old Bearded Man*, a work of fine chromatic quality signed on the back by **Giuseppe Nogari** and dated 1750, evidently based on the Rembrandt models that were much in vogue in Venice in the mid-eighteenth century.

Bernardo Strozzi
Portrait of Cardinal Federico Corner

Three notable seventeenth-century portraits take up the facing wall. On the left is a *Portrait of an Old Woman* by **Pietro Bellotti** of Brescia, typified by the crude realism of the image and the cold, luminous light and datable to the mid-seventeenth century. In the middle is a portrait of *Cardinal Federico Corner* by the Genoese priest, **Bernardo Strozzi**, in which the fluent touch typical of the Flemish tradition in which Strozzi was trained in his home city emerges, along with the extremely vibrant colouristic style that derives from the great sixteenth-century Veneto tradition. Corner was appointed patriarch of Venice in 1631 and remained in office until 1744 when he moved to the papal court in Rome. Critics agree that this portrait of him was painted immediately after the Genoese artist's arrival in Venice in 1633. The series is completed by a *Portrait of a Gentleman in a Wig* by the Friuli artist, **Sebastiano Bombelli**, datable to between 1665 and 1668.

The next section of wall is dedicated to an interesting anthology of paintings by the main landscape artists working in Venice during the eighteenth century. The 'founder' of Venetian landscape painting is unanimously considered to be the Belluno painter **Marco Ricci**, nephew of the celebrated decorator Sebastian. He, too, was famous for his work on theatre scenery and had the opportunity to study the works of Salvator Rosa during his youthful stay in Rome. Marco was able to meld his own learning, based on the Veneto landscape tradition dating back to Titian, to this font of inspiration that was fundamental to the development of his poetic art. Two small canvases by Marco Ricci are exhibited: *Washerwomen on a Riverbank* and *Riders and Monks in a Hilly Area*. The restoration of these works has allowed their remarkable colouristic and compositional quality to be recovered and to confirm that they date from his early career, at the turn of the seventeenth century, as shown by his continued use of fairly dark colours.

The Tuscan **Francesco Zuccarelli** and **Giuseppe Zais** from Agordo were active after the middle of the century, in a different cultural context dominated by the poetic art of Arcadia, at least with regard to the field of landscape painting. The large *Pastoral* by Zuccarelli – repository of an extremely refined style, rich in delicate surface vibrations in line with the tastes of the time – is an elegant representation of great freshness and naturalness; while the four *Landscapes with Peasants* by Zais – more spontaneous and realistic in his figuration – are characterised by the immediacy of the brushwork and the more realistic portrayal of the characters.

Four recently restored oval portraits in stuccoes above the doors giving access to the lateral rooms of the *portego* are also of considerable interest. Above the door leading to the Longhi Room is a portrait of a *Gentleman in Red* by **Niccolò Cassana**; above the door leading to the Parlour Room is a portrait of *Senator Giacomo Correr*, also datable to the early eighteenth century but not easily attributable; above the door leading to the Guardi Room that of *Senator Giovanni Correr*, which may be attributable to **Antonio Bellucci**; and, finally, above the door leading to the rooms where the Zianigo villa has been reconstructed is a portrait of a very elegant noblewoman, identified as *Giustina Renier Donà*. This is attributed to the Brescian painter **Ludovico Gallina**, who probably painted it from memory at least thirty years after the death of the woman in 1751.

The furnishings of the *portego* consist of four simple walnut sofas, six rattan chairs, four stands and an elegantly shaped walnut sideboard.

The next corridor leads from the painting portico to the frescoes from the Zianigo villa.

View of the Punchinellos Room

The next part of the museum is given over to the extraordinary kaleidoscope of frescoes by **Giandomenico Tiepolo** from the still-standing villa in Zianigo, near Mirano, previously owned by the painter's family.

Restored in 1999-2000 by Ottorino Nonfarmale, thanks to a generous contribution from The Venice International Foundation, the frescoes were painted by Giandomenico over a fairly long period of time: between 1759 – the date shown on one of the monochrome scenes from the chapel – and 1797 – according to a now lost inscription read at the beginning of the twentieth century in a mural scene in the Punchinello Room. Almost all the frescoes in the small Zianigo villa were detached in 1906 by Franco Steffanoni to be sold in France by the antiques dealer Antonio Salvadori. But their export was blocked by the Ministry of Education and they were bought partly by the Comune di Venezia and partly by the Italian Government. Some were exhibited in the Correr Museum, but in 1936 they were moved to the Ca' Rezzonico and placed in small rooms created out of two larger halls, in a recomposition that closely repeats the original one, though with some differences and overlapping.

The frescoes depicting the stories of Punchinello, scenes of villa life, games, the wars and affections of satyrs and fauns are one of the most fascinating and singular features of the entire Ca' Rezzonico, while also providing a tail-end view of the eighteenth century in Venice. This is a comprehensive cycle which Giandomenico, then old and certainly marginalised by the new pictorial and decorative fashions of the time, painted for himself in successive stages in the non-monumental rooms of the country house his father had bought on his return from the task of decorating the Prince-Bishop's palace in Würzburg and which he had restored and altered to his own needs. When completed, the whole Zianigo work was a kind of grand recapitulation of many aspects and idiosyncrasies of Giandomenico's art, while also representing the cultural passing of a period and a style. It is almost a pictorial testament which, while valuing the past, did not conceal the drama of the present nor the uncertainty of the future. Indeed, the frescoes were completed by Giandomenico in the lee of events leading up to the end of the Venetian Republic (1797) and the first foreign occupation. But he was able to look at all this with an undeceived and ironic, or even sarcastic, eye, catching, in the frailty of men, also their sorrowful features, the passing of styles and fashions, of passions and hopes, and the survival of a primordial, instinctive will (if not joyful eagerness) to live and to look ahead.

CORRIDOR

In the entrance corridor is the scene showing *Rinaldo leaving the garden of Armida*, taken from *Gerusalemme Liberata* by Torquato Tasso. This fresco was originally on the ground floor of the Zianigo villa, along with other monochromes now exhibited in the Centaurs' Room, and can be dated to immediately after Giandomenico's return from Madrid in November 1770. Inspired by a similar painting by his father, it is marked by an almost caricature style, already emptied of the heroic-mythical *allure* of Giambattista's work. The theme is thus heroic and sentimental, exactly like Tasso's poem and many of Giambattista's figures. But the impassioned and melancholy atmosphere of the episode is already breaking up, revealing

that Giandomenico is doffing his hat as illustrator of poems to replace it with that of the comedian and, even, of the mocking scoffer: the sentimental will still be there, but it will arise from the painter's more general state of mind and be one of the supporting elements of his discourse, one of the well-springs of his inspiration.

On the end wall is the scene of the *Kestrel*, diving onto a flock of fleeing sparrows; almost a snapshot in the realism and immediacy of its depiction. In the Villa this fresco was in a small side room off the *portego*, which was entirely given over to pictures of animals, including two decorations above the doors with images of camels that have been lost, probably after being detached, and the delightful image of the multi-coloured *Parrot* now exhibited above the door to the next rooms.

Giandomenico Tiepolo
Parrot

Giandomenico Tiepolo
Rinaldo leaving the garden of Armida

In the same corridor, on the wall facing the scene of Rinaldo, are three canvases that were not part of the decorations in the Zianigo villa, but are in any case of considerable interest. The two at the bottom show the *Rape of the Sabines* and *Achilles in Scyros*. These were in the past attributed to Giulio Carpioni or the workshop of Gregorio Lazzarini, but are more probably by **Nicolò Bambini**, as the results of the recent restoration have confirmed, due to the type of figures and the high-key of the colouring, which reappear much the same in the works by this painter that definitely date from the end of the seventeenth century or the beginning of the eighteenth.

Above them there is a lunette of very fresh chromatic quality by **Francesco Fontebasso**, a student of Sebastiano Ricci and subsequently particularly attentive to Tiepolo's work. The canvas, which came from the Palazzo Farsetti, shows the *Virgin and Child* seated

among the clouds, worshipped by a young, very elegantly dressed woman symbolising Venice. On the left there is the imposing figure of Mark the evangelist, protector of the city. The painting thus takes on a precise meaning, aimed at highlighting the relationship between the Venetians and the Virgin. This was fairly vibrant in official piety, but even more so in the people's devotion and was always invoked at times of greatest danger, such as wars and plague. It is common opinion that the painting dates from the end of the 1720s and was painted by Fontebasso immediately after his return to Venice following his stay in Rome, where in 1728 he received important recognition from the local Accademia di San Luca.

PASSAGE

The elegant figure of *Abundance* is displayed in the short passage leading to the other rooms given over to Giandomenico Tiepolo's Zianigo works. *Abundance* is presented as a false statue in a painted niche, which was originally on the landing of the staircase between the ground and first floors in the villa, along with other images (some lost). It is quite likely that this work was also part of a series of frescoes painted in the villa immediately after Giandomenico's return from Madrid in November 1770.

Giandomenico Tiepolo
Kestrel

Giandomenico Tiepolo
Abundance

The passage leads on to the main room

THE 'MONDO NOVO' PORTICO

The frescoes in this room – apart from the *Female Head* in monochrome on a red background above the entrance door, which was originally in the chapel entrance – were originally in the ground floor *portego* of the villa and include some of the most celebrated pieces from this cycle.

On the longer side is the *New World*, signed and dated 1791. This highly evocative scene shows a small crowd of country and city folk mixed with nobles (but there is also a curious Punchinello, with a dumpling impaled on a pitchfork) seen from behind, waiting to look into the viewfinder of a magic lantern, a kind of cosmorama or diorama, to see scenes and pictures of far-off countries (precisely, the New World). The scene is laden with singular and disturbing meanings to modern eyes: the expectation of an event, the almost total lack of faces, the metaphysical simplicity of the landscape and the stall of the huckster (standing on the stool) make this one of the most emblematic and charming examples of the awareness of the imminent end of a world, and of the curious bewilderment about a future announced in signs and clues that are still difficult to read.

Some have suggested that the only two figures shown in profile, on the right, are portraits of Tiepolo the father, with arms folded and ironic, penetrating features, and his son further back with the eye-glass.

In front of the *New World* are two sections with the *Minuet in Villa* and the *Promenade*. From the same period and stylistically similar to the former, these are elegant, ironic portrayals of the typical pastimes of the nobility while holidaying in their villas. If the *Prome-*

Giandomenico Tiepolo
Mondo novo

nade seems to herald the preparations for a departure on the part of the Venetian nobility, a leave-taking which does not forego a last wink by the youth on the left who looks back, the *Minuet* cannot but impress with its ironic underlining in the face of ridiculous and vacuous formality, with its emphasis on the transient nature of fashions and behaviours.

In these works Giandomenico probably wanted to give 'live' testimony of the atmosphere of anxious expectation that he too – having in the meantime established residence in the small village of Zianigo – experienced in the years immediately preceding the fall of the Republic of Venice: the decline of the upper class, which had for almost a millennium supported the Venetian oligarchy and was now passively accepting the progressive break-up of the state, continuing with the fatuous ceremonies of villa life, and concern at what would inevitably happen after the now imminent fall of the Serenissima, to know exactly what 'new world' would then take shape.

The ceiling with the *Triumph of the Arts* is much earlier than the wall frescoes and can be dated to the first stage of the Villa's decoration,

prior to 1762 when Giandomenico followed his father to Madrid. The painting is fairly conventional, especially its theme, but the colouristic range of soft tones – recovered during its restoration – is of extraordinary quality. The four terra verde monochrome decorations above the doors, also from the ground floor hall of Zianigo, are instead from the same period as the New World and the other wall frescoes, though thematically linked to the ceiling (*Astronomy, The Faun's Family, Sacrifice with the Heathens, Pyre*). Nature and culture seem to be contrasted in this contorted cycle of figures, half-way between the allegoric-symbolic and the realistic, in which there is perhaps some move from wildness to civilisation, and towards a new dimension of uncorrupted ingenuity (the new world) which the old world looks to, astonished or doubtfully sceptical as the case may be.

Giandomenico Tiepolo
Promenade

Giandomenico Tiepolo
Minuet in villa

THE PUNCHINELLO ROOM

The room that opens up on the right of the New World has frescoes showing scenes from the life of Punchinello that were originally in a small side room off the *portego* in the villa. The three big wall scenes show *Punchinello and the Acrobats, Punchinello in Love* and *Punchinello's Departure*; on the ceiling (the place normally devoted to apparitions of gods or heroes) is the very famous oval with *The Punchinellos' Swing*, surrounded by eight other figures painted on an orange-red background with episodes from the daily life of the stock Neapolitan characters. Other scenes with Punchinello appear in the smaller chiaroscuri: the *Cavalcade of Punchinellos* and the *Dogs' Ballet* in the two overdoors, *Punchinellos driving out a young noblewoman* and *Punchinellos strolling under an umbrella* in the two larger paintings at the sides of the scene with *Punchinello and the Acrobats*. Above the fireplace is another fresco representing *Punchinellos playing with dogs*, while the hood of the fireplace con-

Giandomenico Tiepolo
Punchinellos strolling under an umbrella

sists of a canvas representing a *Greyhound*, of elegant workmanship, also from the villa in Zianigo. The frescoes in this room were painted between 1793, the date that was read in one of the corner scenes of the ceiling before detachment, and 1797, which appears in the section with *Punchinello in Love*. The figure of Punchinello takes on a particular role in them. He is a symbol of that part of humanity that still retains a primordial, spontaneous will to survive in the face of a society in rapid dissolution. So it is no longer the nobles, who in the minor frescoes of the *portego* seem to be shown in the gauche postures of the latest dance or, while strolling, literally leave the stage, but a new, different people: free, equal and all brothers, in deference, it would seem, to the watchwords then coming from revolutionary France. It is no mere chance that in these frescoes the Punchinellos, who have suddenly emerged from the bowels of the earth, through a hole, making use of a ladder, as can be seen in the ceiling, perform actions much the same as those performed by the nobility, though in a much more truculent and vulgar fashion. They amuse themselves with the swing, court women during carnival, watch the acrobats' show, carouse and get drunk, they go strolling and, in one of the monochromes, even chase off a young women dressed in the latest fashion. Here they become the stars of the 'new world', taking over from the old guard, or the nobility with no

Giandomenico Tiepolo
Punchinello's Swing

future who appear in the *portego* pictures. In these frescoes Giandomenico provides a chilling reply to the nobility, the middle class,
the working people and country folk who are anxious to find out
about the 'new world': the old world no longer exists, in its place
there is now the new world of the Punchinellos.

Returning to the portego *of the* New World, *the door on the left of the
main fresco leads to the room where the chapel has been reconstructed.*

Giandomenico Tiepolo
Punchinello in Love

Giandomenico Tiepolo
Punchinello's Departure

CHAPEL

The chapel is to the left of the Zianigo villa facade. The frescoes decorating this small room were probably the first done in the villa by Giandomenico. Indeed, the chapel was dedicated in 1758 to St Jerome Emiliani, the founder of the Somaschan order to which the painter's younger brother, Giuseppe Maria, belonged. It was probably he who suggested the iconography for the fresco. The scene with St Jerome reciting the rosary is dated 1759 beside the signature of Giandomenico.

The circular altar piece carries the delicate image of the *Virgin and Child worshipped by St Jerome Emiliani and St James the apostle*; at the sides, above the doors, are two monochrome Old Testament scenes: *The Sacrifice of Melchizedec* and *Moses Breaking the Tablets of the Law*. Two splendid monochromes dedicated to episodes from the life of the saint – *St Jerome Emiliani striking water from a rock* and *St Jerome Emiliani reciting the rosary* before youths gathered in prayer – occupy the longer walls.

St Jerome Emiliani is again shown in the arched canvas (IRE loan) with the usual shackles recalling the imprisonment of this Venetian nobleman by imperial troops in 1511, from which he was freed by the miraculous intervention of the Virgin. This work is confirmed as being by Giandomenico, contrary to the persistent tendency of critics to refer it to his father Giambattista. The remaining furnishings of the Chapel are further examples of eighteenth-century Venetian crafts.

Returning through the portego, *the door on the left of the corridor leads to the Centaurs Room.*

Giandomenico Tiepolo
St Jerome Emiliani striking water from a rock

Giandomenico Tiepolo
Virgin and Child worshipped by St Jerome Emiliani and St James the Apostle

Giandomenico Tiepolo
St Jerome Emiliani reciting the rosary

CENTAURS ROOM / SATYRS ROOM

The Centaurs Room takes us back to pagan and mythological themes. The ceiling has a red monochrome *Rhapsode* (possibly a Homage to Homer), signed and dated 1791, while the several grey monochrome tondi showing episodes from the life of centaurs and satyrs and one with a *Heathen Sacrifice* are probably from about twenty years earlier.

More satyrs and bacchanalian scenes, historical and mythological events and allegorical figures populate the walls and ceiling of the subsequent Satyrs Room. On the ceiling is a big rectangular frieze with *Scenes of Roman History*, dated 1759, while the other monochrome scenes date from 1771, which is marked on the section with the *Bacchanale of Satyrs and Satyresses*. The other two wall monochromes show the *Satyr's Swing* (this scene predates the one painted twenty years later in the Punchinello Room) and a *Centaur abducting a Satyress*; the decorations above the doors, with a stucco leonine head in the centre, also have images of satyrs and satyresses.

The Harpsichord Room is on the left after coming out of the Zianigo villa rooms.

Giandomenico Tiepolo
Rhapsode

Giandomenico Tiepolo
Heathen Sacrifice

Giandomenico Tiepolo
*Bacchanale of Satyrs
and Satyresses*

Giandomenico Tiepolo
Centaur abducting a Satyress

The setting of a country villa built for the holidays of rich Venetian families has been reconstructed here with furniture from the Villa Mattarello in Arzignano, near Vicenza. The two big wardrobes, each with two doors, are decorated with *Allegories of the Four Seasons* in tempera chiaroscuro on pink tones, in a style recalling that of **Giuseppe Nogari**. The doors are decorated with farming and hunting scenes, also in tempera with similar shades.

A rare example of an early eighteenth-century harpsichord, its three legs richly carved and gilded, is also on display in the middle of the room. The decorations on the sides are in 'poor lacquer', consisting of cut-out prints – in this case, scenes of hunting, landscapes and amorous meetings – pasted onto the surface then covered over with a layer of transparent, protective varnish. The chest of drawers with flap against the wall is decorated in the same way.

Two interesting paintings are also displayed in the room. The first, showing the *Feast of Abigail and Nabal*, is one of the many collaborative works by the figure painter **Francesco Zugno**, who painted the lively figures, and the perspective painter **Francesco Battaglioli**, who designed the impressive architecture framing the scene. The second, which came from the Istituto delle Zitelle at the Giudecca, is a devotional painting framing a sixteenth-century icon by a Madonna painter of Byzantine background. This older image is surrounded by the figures of *Saints Joseph and John* placed against a landscape seen in the warm light of sunset and accompanied by some cherubs, by the Belluno artist **Gaspare Diziani**.

The small passage from the Harpsichord Room gives access to the Parlour Room.

View of the room

Francesco Zugno
Francesco Battaglioli
Feast of Abigail and Nabal

Several small but very interesting paintings are displayed in this narrow corridor. On the wall between the windows is a painting by **Pietro Longhi** showing *The Hairdressed*, giving the last touches to the coiffure of a lady, who is meanwhile chatting with a guest, to whom a servant is offering a tray of fruit. A late work, the painting can be dated around 1760, if not later.

There are two oval-shaped views by **Giuseppe Zais** beside the doors: a *Landscape with Peasant Women* and a *Sea Storm*. These are early works by this unaffected Agordo painter that seem to show signs of influence by Guardi, while the notably bright, clear colouring is typical of Zais.

On the long wall there is a Guardi painting whose attribution has long divided critics: the *Sign of the Art of the Coroneri* (manufacturers of diadems, rosaries and buttons) from the Palazzo dei Camerlenghi at the Rialto where, like the others in the series now kept in the Correr Museum, it was used as a sign for the notice board on which announcements relating to the Art were displayed. The work was commissioned by the steward of the Art, Salvador Ceolino, and completed in 1750 as shown by the inscription at bottom right. The coats of arms at the top are those of the incumbent magistrates of the Giustizia Vecchia, who supervised the activities of the Arts. The canvas has been variously attributed to Gian Antonio and to Francesco Guardi, or considered a work of collaboration by both

brothers: in this case the figures would be by Francesco – a delightful foretaste of the characters in his view-paintings – and the upper part with the coats of arms in elegant rococo style by Antonio. Attribution has more recently favoured **Francesco Guardi** alone, due to the close relationship between this painting and the *Parlour* and the *Ridotto*, now unanimously recognised as his work. However, the hypothesis that the upper part of the painting may have been inspired by the work of his older brother, in whose workshop he was employed in those years, remains compelling.

Two other important small paintings hang on the same wall: a *Pastoral Scene* by **Francesco Zuccarelli**, almost a sketch for a larger work given its size and exceptional compositional freshness, and a *View of Castel Cogolo* by **Francesco Guardi**, painted in 1778 during a trip to Mastellina in Val di Sole where his family was from. Unfortunately not in a particularly good state of preservation, the small canvas can be connected to the drawing of a similar subject in the Museo Correr. The splendid torch-holder in Murano glass, probably by **Giuseppe Briati**, which was part of the bequest from the engineer Giuseppe Gatti Casazza (1962), is displayed in the niche in the same wall.

Giuseppe Zais
Landscape with Peasant Women

Giuseppe Zais
Storm

Francesco Guardi
Sign of the Art of the Coroneri

Two of the most celebrated canvases by **Francesco Guardi** are displayed here, one in front of the other: *The parlour of the nuns of San Zaccaria* and *The Ridotto at Palazzo Dandolo in San Moisè*. The attributive vicissitudes of these Guardi masterpieces are well-known. Along with the canvases in the Chiesa dell'Angelo Raffaele in Venice, they have for many years been the centre of the dispute between scholars of eighteenth-century Venetian art, aimed at reconstructing the artistic personality and individual catalogues of the two Guardi brothers, Antonio and Francesco. The paintings came to the museum from the Correr collection with an enigmatic attribution to 'Guardi'. In the nineteenth century they were long considered to be by Pietro Longhi, and only from the beginning of the twentieth, with the renewed interest in the work of the Guardis, were they alternatively attributed to Francesco or Antonio, or else considered works of collaboration by both. Only recently has the certainty been reached that they are early works by the younger of the two brothers. This attribution was aided by their comparison with two canvases of similar subject in the Heinemann collection in New York – one of which, the *Anteroom of the Great Council*, which has a *Ridotto* quite similar to that in the Ca' Rezzonico as a companion piece, is signed by Francesco Guardi. They may be dated to the second half of the 1740s, in the period when Francesco was paying particular attention to the works of Pietro Longhi, from which he derived some of the many figures present in the *Parlour*.

Bartolomeo Nazari
Portrait of Samuel Egerton

These two 'interior views' therefore in some respects precede those splendid city views Francesco began producing only from the end of the following decade. Indeed, the extremely lively figures show the same freshness of touch and the same lightness of colour as those populating his numerous views of Venice.

The *Ridotto* shows the grand hall of the gaming house in the Palazzo Dandolo in San Moisè, lined with *cuoridoro*, as it was prior to 1768 when the interior of the old building was refurbished in neoclassical style to a design by Bernardino Maccaruzzi. The *Parlour*, on the other hand, shows the visiting room at the San Zaccaria monastery, one of the most important in Venice, where the descendants of the most noble Venetian families were sent to become nuns. Relatives and friends could talk to the nuns here, and on these occasions puppet shows were also organised for the children.

In addition to these two masterpieces, other paintings of considerable interest are displayed in this room. The *Parlour* is flanked by two portraits by **Pietro Longhi**: on the left is that of *Andrea Benedetto*

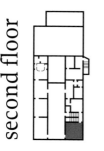

second floor

118

Ganassoni, Bishop of Feltre, dated 1774 on the back and possibly painted at the same time as the large portrait painted in the same year by his son Alessandro, now in the Seminary at Feltre; on the right the *Portrait of a Painter*, signed and dated 1781, which is perhaps a likeness of Alessandro, but is certainly one of the last works by Pietro, who died in 1785. Two more paintings by Longhi are displayed at the sides of the large mirror on the wall facing the windows overlooking the Grand Canal: on the right is an *Nursemaid*, on the left a *Fainting*. These are both early works by the master, given that references to Crespi's teachings are still evident, datable to around 1740, heralding the series painted for the Veniers in 1741, now in the Gallerie dell'Accademia di Venezia.

The two 'models' alongside the *Ridotto* are by different artists. On the left is a preparatory work by **Giambattista Tiepolo** for an altar piece that was perhaps never produced, depicting the *Martyrdom of St Theodora*. The restoration of this work has fully recovered its colour-

Giambattista Tiepolo
Martyrdom of St Theodora

Francesco Guardi
*The parlour of the nuns
of San Zaccaria*

overleaf:
View of the room

ing, confirming its attribution despite the doubts expressed in the past, though this is also evident in the stenographic brushwork and expert synthesis of sign so typical of Giambattista. On the right is the model for the *Portrait of Samuel Egerton* by **Bartolomeo Nazari**, now in Tatton Park, England. It has significant differences to the larger version, lacking the view of the Salute and part of the Giudecca in the background and being incomplete in the detail of the paving and the staircase baluster. This is most likely a rapid sketch, done from life by Nazari in 1728 when Samuel Egerton was in Venice as a guest of the English consul, Joseph Smith, and subsequently used to paint the portrait sent to England.

An oval portrait of *Marco Foscarini* hangs between the windows

overlooking the Grand Canal. This future doge is shown with pen in hand beside his books, recalling his work as the official historian of the Republic between 1732 and 1735. The canvas was in the past attributed to the Neapolitan Corrado Giaquinto, but subsequent studies have shown that it was painted by the French artist **Pierre Subleyras** in Rome at the end of the 1730s, during Foscarini's last years there as Venetian ambassador to the papal court.

A fresco removed from the Palazzo Nani in Cannaregio was adapted for the ceiling in the 1930s. It portrays *Marital Accord* crowned by Virtue in the presence of Justice, Prudence, Temperance, Fame, Abundance and Divinity, with views of villas and gardens at the sides and monochrome putti with scrolls at the corners. It was tra-

Francesco Guardi
*The Ridotto at palazzo Dandolo
in San Moisè*

ditionally considered the only figure work by the Ferrara *trompe-l'oeil* artist Gerolamo Mengozzi, called Colonna, Tiepolo's faithful associate who also worked for the Nani family, though some believed it to be by Jacopo Guarana. The fresco, in fairly poor condition – also due to the manner in which it was detached – has only recently been more plausibly attributed to the late eighteenth-century decorator **Costantino Cedini** and dated to around 1790.

The furniture in yellow-green lacquer with floral decorations, originally from the Palazzo Calbo Crotta agli Scalzi, is of very high quality. The big chest of drawers stands out in particular with its curved line and marble top, crowned by the impressive but slender mirror with very fine gilt crest. The same *rocaille* line is also evident in the

two matching side tables, and repeated in the ten elegant armchairs (the upholstery is modern). The presser-foot frame surrounding the wall coverings (also modern) is also quite original. The fine, lacquered, double-wing door with light green background and gilt borders and carving, decorated with imaginary scenes and polychrome floral elements, is also from the Palazzo Calbo Crotta.

The Longhi Room is reached by returning across the portego.

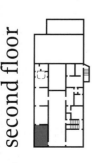

The corner room between the Grand Canal and the Rio di San Barnaba, which corresponds to the big Throne Room on the first *piano nobile*, may provide the grounds for an original comparison between two different aspects of the Venetian eighteenth century: the mythological-allegorical, lively and sensual character of the rococo in the oval ceiling canvas by **Giambattista Tiepolo**, with *Zephyrus and Flora*, and the Venetian version of the rational, questioning, ironic and incisive, critical self-consciousness of the age of enlightenment in the 'genre' canvases of Pietro Longhi, which line the walls, offering a detailed and enriching study of the daily, elegant face of the city.

The canvas depicting the *Triumph of Zephyrus and Flora* came from its original site in one of the rooms on the *piano nobile* of the Ca' Pesaro. It is one of Giambattista's early works, within the first half of

the 1730s, having been painted for the wedding of Antonio Pesaro and Caterina Sagredo in 1732. The presence of both Zephyrus – one of the four winds in pagan mythology – and Flora – goddes of flowers – clearly alludes to the rebirth of the land, to spring and therefore also to fertility. The colours are brilliant and transparent; elements of undoubted prowess, such as Flora's iridescent drapery and the crystalline, mother-of-pearl transparency of Zephyrus' and the cherubs' wings, alternate with the sensual rendering of the skin tones, the pleasing contrast of chromatic elements and intonations (note Zephyrus' hand on Flora's armpit). Although ethereal and 'spontaneous', the scene is skilfully constructed: the balance of the two floating bodies is provided by the play of raised and outspread arms and by the splayed legs

Pietro Longhi
Portrait of Francesco Guardi

Giambattista Tiepolo
Triumph of Zephyrus and Flora

in the bottom-up view. What seems unusual is rather a certain melancholy in the faces and expressions of the lovers, which contrasts with the festive spring reawakening to which the canvas alludes. There is an absence of enthusiasm and joy, as if in a theatrical, scenographic montage, where everything seems to occur according to an established script rather than celebrating a vital explosion and a renewal of nature.

The twenty-eight canvases with genre scenes by **Pietro Longhi** in the room (all recently cleaned and restored) offer a significant example of this painter's art. Amorous meetings and the daily life of rich nobles and humble peasants appear, along with visits to the painter's studio and the hairdresser at work, household conversation and 'exotic and monstrous' curiosities, family groups and little concerts: in short, a grand repertoire of situations and contexts, of everyday incidents and pleasures. Beyond the agreeable nature of

126

Pietro Longhi
*Conversation between
Dominoes*

Pietro Longhi
The Perfume Seller

Pietro Longhi
The Fortune Teller

Pietro Longhi
Exhibition of the Rhinoceros

overleaf:
View of the room

129

Pietro Longhi
The Friar's Visit

Pietro Longhi
Family Concert

Pietro Longhi
Venetian Noble Family

Rosalba, which are quite close to his elegant use of colour – consistent with themselves and reflective, intent as they are on a substantial economy of signs and words to conduct their own highly eloquent artistic discourse.

The paintings are not shown in chronological order, but grouped by subject. However, they do allow the development of Longhi's art to be identified. His genre scenes started from the example of the Bologna painter Giuseppe Maria Crespi, whose works Pietro saw during a stay in Bologna, probably in the early 1730s. The four pictures with popular images (*The Spinners*, *The Washerwomen*, *The Happy Couple*, *The Polenta*) displayed at the sides of the fireplace underneath a large mirror, on the wall facing the Rio di San Barnaba, are marked by the brown tone of the background and date from his closest approach to the Crespi world, at the end of that decade.

In about 1740 Pietro Longhi decidedly lightened his palette, on models of the Venetian rococo. Many of the works shown here belong to this period, such as the highly celebrated *Painter's Studio*, with the very elegant lady, accompanied by a ladies' man, having her portrait painted, or *The Horse-ride*, one of Longhi's rare pictures *en plein air*.

The painter's main masterpieces date from the '50s, and of those at the Ca' Rezzonico, note must be made in particular of the lively image of the *Moor delivering a letter to a lady*, the one dedicated to the *Exhibition of the Rhinoceros*, painted on commission in 1751 for Giovanni Grimani to record the arrival of a rhinoceros in Venice from India during the carnival of that year, the enigmatic *Conversation between Dominoes* in a Venice square, *The Fortune Teller*, *The Perfume Seller* and the brilliant *Family Concert*, with the Bohemian musician Giacomo Scumar, quite famous in his time, intent on brightening up the day for an old lady and her daughters. The fine group portrait of a *Venetian Noble Family*, notable for its colouring on light tones, rich in shading, and the curious *Portrait of the Giant Cornelio Magrat*, a young Irishman who came to Venice in 1757, 'seven feet tall and weighing 420 pounds', as noted in the inscription, belong to this same period.

Other famous paintings date from the following decade, such as the scene of the *Hairdresser* and that of the *Friar's Visit*. The *Morning Chocolate*, marked by the more quavering brushstroke found in the Venetian painter's later works dates rather from the end of the 1770s.

The fine furnishings in yellow lacquer with decorations of red volutes and flowers were originally part of the furniture in a hall at the Palazzo Calbo Crotta. The rare semi-circular sofa is particularly striking.

Pietro Longhi
Painter's Studio

The room known as the Green Lacquer Room is certainly one of the most evocative in the building. It takes its name from the dark green lacquered furniture with decorative elements in gilt moulded plaster, which came from the Palazzo Calbo Crotta in Cannaregio. Chests of drawers, mirrors with elegant floral crests, small chairs, *consoles* and stands: all are similarly and elegantly designed and decorated in accordance with an eighteenth-century style that can be dated to the 1750s. The theme of the decoration is inspired by the oriental chinoiserie style that had been so popular in Venice, too, in the major arts (as in Giandomenico Tiepolo's frescoes in the Villa Valmarana) in fine crafts, in fashion and in the style of furnishing and decoration. Pagodas, umbrellas, willows, cherry trees and oriental figurines in gold all drift over the charming green lacquer background, set amid curls of rocaille frames, generous festoons and floral carving, once again proposing a Venetian idea of a mythical, imagined Orient, reflecting the stories of Carlo Gozzi and confined to a dimension without time or history.

The polychrome figures of Chinese people with moveable heads shown on the chests, in lacquered papier mâché, are of eighteenth-century oriental origin.

Some views of Venice and two landscapes are displayed in the room. The wall on the right of the entrance from the Longhi Room is devoted to the latter: the fine *Landscape with Shepherd Boys* is a typical late work by **Giuseppe Zais**, while the *Landscape with Bridge* and a small village in the background, marked by its mellow colours, is by **Antonio Diziani**, son of the more renowned Gaspare who specialised in this type of painting.

Antonio Diziani
Landscape with Bridge

Antonio Guardi
Triumph of Diana

overleaf:
View of the room

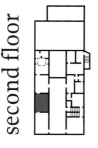

The picture by a late follower of Battaglioli on the wall nearby is particularly interesting. It shows *The Frozen Lagoon*, and refers to the big freeze that hit Venice in 1788, as can be seen in the inscription. This covered the waters of the northern lagoon from the Fondamente Nuove to the mainland with a thick layer of ice on which the Venetians even ventured to stroll. The big *View of St Mark's Basin*, seen from the island of San Giorgio Maggiore, with the buildings in the Piazzetta San Marco and the bell-tower on the right and the entrance to the Grand Canal in the middle, dominated by the high dome of the Chiesa della Salute, is by **Vincenzo Chilone**, a view painter active in the seventeenth century who followed Canaletto's models.

Finally, two views showing the *Grand Canal towards the Salute* and the *Grand Canal at San Vio* are displayed on the wall facing the entrance. These can be attributed to a late imitator of Canaletto, though they are not lacking in quality, as confirmed by the fact that they have in the past been attributed to Canaletto himself or to his nephew and pupil, Bernardo Bellotto.

But the most significant picture in the room is probably the fresco on the ceiling surrounded by a modern stucco frame. This is the fine *Triumph of Diana* by **Antonio Guardi**, which makes up a set with his other frescoes shown in the next room, like this one, removed from their original site in the Palazzo Barbarigo-Dabalà at Angelo Raffaele and mounted on canvas. The rocaille style of the allegorical-mythological decorative component in its more Venetian and ethereal inflection, whose most imaginative and refined interpreter was the elder Guardi brother, here gives natural and elegant proof of its possibilities. The picture dates from Antonio's later career, in the 1750s. He evidently took into account the model provided by Sebastiano Ricci's canvas portraying the *Triumph of Wisdom*, which is in the library of the current Patriarchal Seminary in Venice, the old Somaschan convent.

The other three frescoes by **Antonio Guardi** that were removed from their original site in the Palazzetto Dabalà, formerly Barbarigo, at Angelo Raffaele, which make up a set with the one on the ceiling in the Green Lacquer Room, have been positioned on the walls here within specially shaped stucco frames. They portray *Venus*, *Love* and *Apollo and Minerva*.

They were probably commissioned by Maria Savorgnan, the wife of Marc'Antonio Barbarigo, who was head of this branch of the noble family residing in the parish of Angelo Raffaele. The four frescoes were covered with whitewash during the nineteenth century and only rediscovered by chance during some restoration works to the building in 1936. On that occasion they were detached and mounted on canvas and taken to the Ca' Rezzonico. Despite their precarious condition after such treatment, these works – the only frescoes by Guardi to have come down to us – still clearly show his rococo decorative talent, made light and joyous by the use of soft, almost pastel colours, and by the characteristic 'open' forms of his pictorial style. The works are presumably from the same years as the ceiling with *Aurora*, previously in the Cini collection in Venice: the beginning of the 1750s. The contemporary nature of the works is confirmed not only by the very close similarity of style, but also by the fact that the preparatory drawing for the *Minerva*, now in the Spector collection in New York, has one for the *Aurora* on its other side.

The furnishings consist of green lacquered pieces decorated with polychrome flowers, bequeathed by the Savorgnan Brazzà family. There are nine armchairs with curved legs and backs, gilt carving and early twentieth-century, white satin upholstery with floral motifs, and two, small, elegantly rounded chests of drawers with doors and opening tops.

The fireplace in red Verona marble, from the Palazzo Carminati in San Stae, has original stuccoes in delicate chromatic tones on the cowl and the figure of *Abundance* portrayed in an oval at the centre. The elegant chandelier of faceted crystal drops and polichrome flowers is a late eighteenth-century piece from Murano in imitation of similar works from Bohemia.

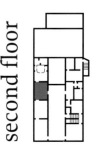

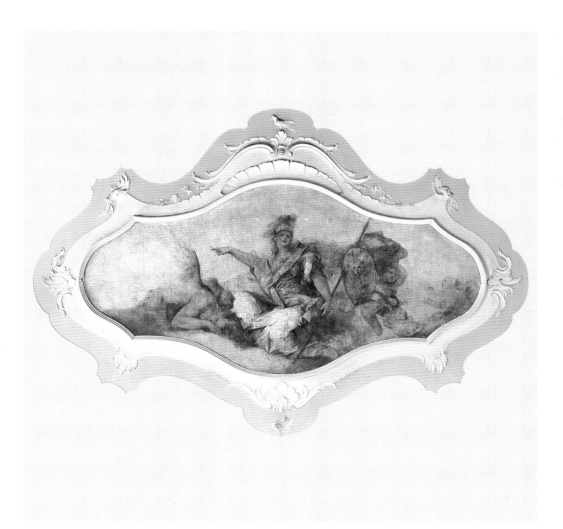

Antonio Guardi
Minerva

Seventeenth-century Venetian Art
Bureau in green laquer decorated with polychrome flowers

143

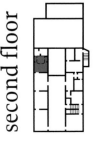

A bedroom has been reconstructed in this room and the small subsequent rooms, complete with dressing rooms, wardrobe and small *boudoir.*

The alcove, which takes up almost half of the main room, came from the Palazzo Carminati in San Stae. It encloses the bed within an ivory-white painted, carved, wooden structure whose mock-classical lines date it to the second half of the eighteenth century. The bed has a shaped wooden headboard, painted in tempera, with a *Sacred Family with St Anne and St Joachim* in the centre. A *Madonna* by **Rosalba Carriera** in pastel played out on the shaded light-blue tones

Rosalba Carriera
Virgin

of her dress and the silver of her veil, datable to the second half of the 1720s, hangs above it in a fine, original, gilt frame. The portrayal of the hands is a rare detail in works by this artist who, as is known from the testimony of her contemporaries, only painted them if the client was willing to pay a substantial surcharge over the agreed price. A small anonymous round canvas in a simple stucco frame on the ceiling portrays a *Virgin and Child.*

Outside the alcove, the furnishings consist of an inlaid bureau-trumeau in walnut root with single mirror door and carved crest, probably of Lombard origin, and a green lacquered cradle with polychrome flowers and neoclassical-style decorations. On the ceiling there is an allegorical painting of the Venetian school from the mid-eighteenth century. The walls are lined with eighteenth-century wallpaper decorated with small landscapes, views of the country, of ruins and figures, in the style of Ricci, printed and finished in brush. It probably came from the Remondini printing works in Bassano.

Two small doors at the sides of the bed, crowned by anonymous female portraits, lead to two parallel corridors. The one on the right has another door that opens onto the alcove and a display case at the end with the precious toilet set previously owned by the Pisani family. This is made up of 58 embossed, engraved items in gilt silver with lavish use of onyx. It comprises the whole *nécessaire* for the lady: from the big table mirror, embossed shell-basin, jewellery case, powder puff, candlesticks and bottles for essences and perfumes, right through to writing equipment and cutlery. The joined coats of arms of the Pisani and Grimani families can be seen on the case on the lower shelf, suggesting the set was a gift for a wedding between members of these two noble families. It is the work of the renowned German craftsmen of Habsburg and dates from the late seventeenth century.

The door to the left of the alcove opens onto another narrow pas-

View of the alcove

sageway, decorated with an oval canvas on the ceiling depicting *Putti in Flight*, in the style of **Jacopo Guarana**. This corridor leads to the room containing the wardrobes, painted in tempera on light shades of grey, green and violet. From here there is access to the innermost Stucco Room, moved here from the Palazzo Calbo Crotta for which it was originally built. It is a more or less octagonal space whose walls are completely lined with the original eighteenth-century polychrome stuccoes, attributed to **Stefano Torelli** from Emilia. These are also the frames for the two big facing mirrors and the four smaller corner ones. The decorations are completed by the illusionistic frescoes on the ceiling, by **Jacopo Guarana**, portraying flying putti and animals in the lunettes, with a cherub and young girls dispensing flowers in the larger central section. There are ovals at the corners of the ceiling with other monochrome figures of putti. The furnishings of the small sitting room consist of a simple sofa and two small chairs in yellow lacquer with floral decorations. Overall, this is a room of refined, typically rococo, elegance, quite worthy of the fame it was already accorded when in its original position.

The 'Ai Do San Marchi' Chemist's Shop, reconstructed here by Nino Barbantini and Giulio Lorenzetti in 1936 with the original furnishings, panelling and instruments, has been kept unchanged on the third floor.

The shop occupied the building on the corner of Calle Donà in Campo San Stin, Venice, until 1908 and there is evidence of its existence from the second half of the seventeenth century. Indeed, it is known that in 1679 its owner was Orazio Moscatello, who at the same time was prior at the Collegio degli Spezieri. Around the middle of the eighteenth century the shop was owned by Bernardo Saletti and supplied medicines to the nearby dei Frari convent. The business had a period of considerable prosperity under Saletti's ownership, such that he was able to completely renovate the rooms. The furnishings and most of the majolica jars and objects in fine Murano glass now in the Ca' Rezzonico date from this period. In 1908 the last owner's widow, Anna Mazzoni in Costa, decided to sell the shop furnishings. These were bought by Raoul Heilbronneur, a Paris antiques dealer, who, prevented from taking them to France, decided to donate the whole set – on the suggestion of the Venetian sculptor Antonio Dal Zotto – to the Musei Civici Veneziani. The furniture and objects were initially displayed in one of the side turrets of the Fondaco dei Turchi, then the home of the Correr Museum, but were then moved to the third floor of the Ca' Rezzonico in 1936.

The Chemist's Shop consists of three communicating rooms. The first, the shop itself, is furnished with an elegant unit in dark walnut root with 183 decorated majolica jars on its shelves for holding the spices and materials used to make up the medicines, made by **Cozzi** of Venice. The two, larger, double-handled jars, placed symmetrically at the corners of the end wall, carry the shop sign: two facing lions holding the open Gospel, the symbol of Mark the Evangelist, patron saint of Venice. The elegant desk with its fine curved lines is also noteworthy.

The second room is taken up by the laboratory, with fireplace and furnace, along with alembics in the most varied of shapes, in gossamer-thin glass made in Murano.

View of the Chemist's Shop

The third room is the 'back room'. The walls here are completely lined with painted pine panelling, enriched with carved capitals and other decorative elements, now returned to its original colour after the recent restoration carried out with the assistance of the French Rallye San Marco association. On the shelves stand 76 decorative, blue-patterned, white majolica jars, evidently part of the shop furnishings before the alterations made by Saletti, and 33 jars in Murano glass. The two big mortars used to pulverise the raw materials are also of interest.

The important Egidio Martini Gallery on the third and fourth floors of the building is reached by returning to the *portego* and ascending the staircase to the left. The gallery offers a comprehensive panorama of Venetian seventeenth- and eighteenth-century painting, comprising 264 masterpieces with works by **Palma il Giovane**, **Padovanino**, **Giulio Carpiani**, **Bernardo Strozzi**, **Francesco Maffei**, **Pietro Vecchia**, **Sebastiano Mazzoni**, **Luca Giordano**, **Pietro Liberi**, **Antonio Balestra**, **Sebastiano** and **Marco Ricci**, **Antonio Marini**, **Giambattista Piazzetta**, **Rosalba Carriera**, **Gian Antonio Pellegrini**, **Jacopo Amigoni**, **Giambattista Tiepolo**, **Giambattista Pittoni**, **Nicola Grassi**, **Gaspare Diziani**, **Bernardino Bison** and the **Ciardi**, along with numerous fifteenth- and sixteenth-century paintings by artists such as **Alvise Vivarini**, **Giambattista Cima**, **Palma il Vecchio**, **Giovanni Cariani**, **Paris Bordon**, **Tintoretto**, **Bonifazio de' Pitati** and **Paolo Fiammingo**. A specific catalogue is dedicated to this exhibition.

The Gallery takes up almost all the space on the third floor of the building, also continuing into the vast area created in the attic. A *Short Guide* and a *Catalogue Raisonné* of the paintings in the gallery have been published.

*View of a room
of the Picture gallery*

The internal staircase leads back to the ground floor of the building. The doorway in front of the exit opens onto a staircase to the mezzanine floor where the collection of paintings donated to the museum in December 2001 by Ferruccio Mestrovich in memory of his family and the destruction of the city of his birth, Zadar, during the Second World War, is housed. The Ferruccio Mestrovich Collection consists of 15 works from the fifteenth to the eighteenth centuries, all of extraordinary quality, and a board for the 'royal game' painted by **Paolo Scorzia**. Particular note must be made of **Jacopo Tintoretto**'s painting, with *Christ taken down from the Cross supported by St John and Mary Magdalene*, in the presence of the sponsors and the *Portrait of Francesco Gherardini*, and of the *Sacred Conversation* by **Bonifazio de' Pitati**. A specific *Guide* to the collection has been published.

View of a room of the Collection

G.J. Fontana, *Cento palazzi fra i più celebri di Venezia...*, Venice 1865.

G. Lorenzetti – L. Planiscig, *La collezione dei conti Donà dalle Rose a Venezia*, Venice 1934.

G. Damerini, *Settecento veneziano in Palazzo Rezzonico*, in 'Le Tre Venezie', 1936.

G. Lorenzetti, *Ca' Rezzonico*, Venice 1936[1].

R. Pallucchini, *La pittura veneziana del Settecento*, Rome 1960.

T. Pignatti, *Il Museo Correr di Venezia. Dipinti del XVII e XVIII secolo*, Venice 1960.

E. Bassi, *Architettura del Sei e Settecento a Venezia*, Naples 1962.

A. Morassi, *A Complete Catalogue of the Paintings of G.B. Tiepolo*, London 1962.

G. Mariacher, *Il restauro della facciata di Ca' Rezzonico*, in 'Bollettino dei Musei Civici Veneziani', 1964.

E. Martini, *La pittura veneziana del Settecento*, Venice 1964.

T. Pignatti, *Tesori di Ca' Rezzonico*, Milan 1965.

G. Mariacher, *Ca' Rezzonico*, Venice 1966.

D. Valeri – G. Mariacher, *Il Settecento a Ca' Rezzonico*, Florence 1966.

A. Pallucchini, *L'opera completa di Giambattista Tiepolo*, Milan 1968.

T. Pignatti, *Pietro Longhi*, Venice 1968.

A. Mariuz, *Giandomenico Tiepolo*, Venice 1971.

A. Massari, *Giorgio Massari architetto veneziano del Settecento*, Vicenza 1971.

G. Pavanello, *Costantino Cedini (1741-1811)*, in 'Bollettino del Museo Civico di Padova', 1972.

A. Morassi, *Guardi. Antonio e Francesco Guardi*, Venice 1973.

M. Guiotto, *Vicende storiche e restauro della Villa Tiepolo a Zianigo di Mirano*, in 'Ateneo Veneto', 1976.

C. Alberici, *Il mobile veneto*, Milan 1980.

E. Noè, *Rezzonicorum cineres. Ricerche sulla collezione Rezzonico*, in 'Rivista dell'Istituto Nazionale di Archeologia e Storia dell'Arte', 1980.

E. Martini, *La pittura del Settecento veneto*, Udine 1982.

L. Puppi, *La gondola del Procuratore. Committenze e peripezie di quattro dipinti del Canaletto*, in 'Bollettino dei Musei Civici Veneziani', 1983-1984.

M. Levey, *Giambattista Tiepolo, his Life and Art*, New Haven and London 1986 (It. ed. 1988).

F. Pedrocco, *Giandomenico Tiepolo a Zianigo*, Treviso 1988.

B. Sani, *Rosalba Carriera*, Turin 1988.

Una città e il suo museo: un secolo e mezzo di collezioni civiche veneziane, n. monografico del 'Bollettino dei Civici Musei Veneziani' (1986), Venice 1988.

P. Rossi, *Francesco Maffei*, Milan 1991.

F. Pedrocco – F. Montecuccoli degli Erri, *Antonio Guardi*, Milan 1992.

M. Gemin – F. Pedrocco, *Giambattista Tiepolo. I dipinti. Opera completa*, Venice 1993.

Pietro Longhi, catalogue of the Venice exhibition, a cura di A. Mariuz, G. Pavanello, G. Romanelli, Milan 1993.

R. Pallucchini, *La pittura nel Veneto. Il Settecento*, Milan 1995-1996, 2 vols.

G. Romanelli – F. Pedrocco, *Ca' Rezzonico*, Milan 1995.

Splendori del Settecento veneziano, catalogue of the Venice exhibition, edited by G. Nepi Scirè, G. Romanelli, Milan 1995.

Giambattista Tiepolo 1696-1996, catalogue of the Venice and New York exhibitions, Milan 1996.

F. Pedrocco, *'700 veneziano. Capolavori da Ca' Rezzonico*, catalogue of the Rome exhibition, Venice 1998.

Satiri, Centauri e Pulcinelli. Gli affreschi restaurati di Giandomenico Tiepolo conservati a Ca' Rezzonico,